단기간에 마무리하는 **8**가지 핵심 비법

비법 담은 중학 영문법

영문법

특강편 **2**

비법 담은 중학 영문법 특강편 2

지은이	한길연, 이나영, 박영은
펴낸이	최회영
책임편집	김종원, 이승혜
감수	정은화, 오승희, 이지애, 이수진, 임미정, 김주희
영문교열	David Charlton
디자인	디자인플러스
펴낸곳	(주)웅진컴퍼스
등록번호	제22-2943호
등록일자	2006년 6월 16일
주소	서울특별시 서초구 강남대로39길 15-10 한라비발디스튜디오193 3층
전화	(02)3471-0096
홈페이지	http://www.wjcompass.com
ISBN	979-11-6237-001-8

12 11 10 9 8
25 24

Photo Credits

All photos © Shutterstock, Inc.

Printed in Korea

CONTENTS

이 책의 구성과 특징

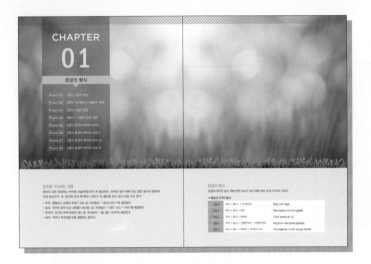

챕터 가이드

각 챕터의 학습 목표, 배울 내용과 함께 중요한 문법의 개념과 용어를 한눈에 보기 쉽도록 정리하였습니다.

핵심만 쏙! 문법 Point

쉽고 정확한 문법 설명과 최신 교과서의 구문을 반영한 실용적인 예문을 제공합니다.

핵심만 콕! 문법 Check

앞서 배운 문법을 다양한 유형의 문제로 풀어보며 다시 한번 확인하도록 합니다.

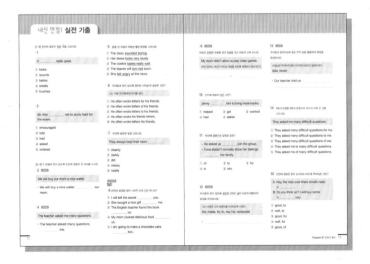

내신 만점! 실전 기출

최근 7년 전국 중학교 기출문제를 최다 빈출 문항 위주로 제공합니다. 또한 비중이 커진 수행평가를 위한 서술형 문제와 고난도 문항까지 완벽 대비합니다.

목차

CHAPTER
01

문장의 형식

문장을 구성하는 성분

영어의 모든 문장에는 주어와 서술어(동사)가 꼭 필요하다. 하지만 동사 뒤에 오는 말은 동사의 종류에 따라
달라진다. 즉, 동사에 따라 목적어나 보어가 꼭 필요할 수도 있고 아닐 수도 있다.

- 주어: 행동이나 상태의 주체가 되는 말. 우리말로 '～은/는/이/가'에 해당한다.
- 동사: 주어의 동작 또는 상태를 나타내는 말. 우리말로 '～하다' 또는 '～이다'에 해당한다.
- 목적어: 동작의 목적/대상이 되는 말. 우리말의 '～을, 를/～에게'에 해당한다.
- 보어: 주어나 목적어를 보충 설명하는 말이다.

한눈에 쏙! 문법 Chart

- **문장의 5가지 형식**

1형식	주어 + 동사 (+ 수식어구)	She runs fast.
2형식	주어 + 동사 + 보어	The music sounds great.
3형식	주어 + 동사 + 목적어	I had lunch at 12.
4형식	주어 + 동사 + 간접목적어 + 직접목적어	He gave me some advice.
5형식	주어 + 동사 + 목적어 + 목적격 보어	The teacher made us go home.

핵심만 쏙! 문법 Point

Point 01 1형식은 주어+동사, 2형식은 주어 + 동사 + 보어로 구성돼요!

- **1형식 문장**: 「주어 + 동사」로만 의미가 완성될 수 있는 문장이다. 보통 수식어구와 함께 쓰인다.
  또한, 존재를 알리는 「There + be동사 + 주어」 구문도 1형식 문장이다. '~이 있다'로 해석한다.
  I walk to school. / There is a big tree in the garden.

- **2형식 문장**: 「주어 + 동사 + 주격 보어」로 의미가 완성될 수 있는 문장이다. 이 때, '주격 보어'란
  주어를 보충 설명해 주는 말로, 명사(구)나 형용사(구)가 온다.
  He became a pianist. / The weather got cold.
  　　　　　주격보어　　　　　　　　　　　　　　　주격보어

- **2형식에 쓰이는 동사**

~이다, (상태가) ~하다	be동사, keep, stay 등
(결과적으로) ~되다	become, get, go, turn 등
감각동사	look, smell, sound, taste, feel 등

Point 02 감각동사 다음에는 형용사가 와요. 부사는 올 수 없어요!

- 「감각동사 (look, smell, sound, taste, feel 등) + 형용사」: ~하게 보이다/냄새가 나다/들리다/
  맛이 나다/느껴지다
  This pillow feels soft. / The cookie smells delicious.
  　　　　　　　형용사(보어)　　　　　　　　　　　형용사(보어)

  > 「감각동사 (look, smell, sound, taste, feel 등) + like + 명사」: ~처럼 보이다/냄새가 나다/
  > 들리다/맛이 나다/느껴지다
  > He looks like his father.

Point 03 3형식은 「주어 + 동사 + 목적어」, 4형식은 「주어 + 동사 + 간접목적어 + 직접목적어」로 구성돼요!

He enjoys playing musical instruments. 그는 악기 연주하는 것을 좋아한다. (3형식)
　　　　　　　　목적어

He bought his girlfriend a ring. 그는 그의 여자친구에게 반지를 사줬다. (4형식)
　　　　　　　　간·목　　　직·목

* 간접목적어는 문장에서 '~에게'로, 직접목적어는 '~을/를'로 해석된다.

Point 04 4형식 문장을 3형식으로 전환할 때는 동사에 따라 전치사를 달리 써요!

to	give, teach, send, bring, show write, tell, lend, pass 등	Jane wrote him a letter. (4형식) → Jane wrote a letter to him. (3형식)
for	make, buy, cook, find, get 등	My mom made us some cookies. (4형식) → My mom made some cookies for us. (3형식)
of	ask, beg 등	Can I ask you a question? (4형식) → Can I ask a question of you? (3형식)

핵심만 콕! 문법 Check

A 괄호 안에서 알맞은 말을 고르시오.

1 He (looked, looked like) sad.　　**2** The girl looks like (scary, a ghost).

3 The food smells (terrible, terribly).　　**4** The shoes (smell, smell like) bad.

5 It (sounds, sounds like) good.　　**6** His vacation plan sounds (good, well).

7 This blanket feels very (soft, softly).　　**8** Your cake (tastes, tastes like) sweet and sour.

B 밑줄 친 부분을 어법에 맞게 고쳐 쓰시오.

1 She looked very <u>nervously</u>.　　→ _____

2 The music sounds <u>strangely</u> to me.　　→ _____

3 This apple pie tastes <u>well</u>.　　→ _____

4 Her new perfume smells <u>greatly</u>.　　→ _____

C 다음 4형식 문장을 〈보기〉와 같이 3형식 문장으로 고쳐 쓰시오.

> **보기**
>
> My older sister taught me Chinese every Saturday.
> → My older sister taught Chinese to me every Saturday.

1 He gave me his email address.

→ _____

2 Julie made me some chocolate.

→ _____

3 Penny asked me a favor.

→ _____

D 우리말과 뜻이 같도록 괄호 안의 말을 바르게 배열하여 문장을 완성하시오.

1 나의 여동생은 내게 맛있는 음식을 만들어 준다. (cooks, my younger sister, me, food, for, delicious)

→ _____

2 나는 그녀에게 약간의 꽃을 사줄 것이다. (will, I, buy, her, flowers, some)

→ _____

핵심만 쏙! 문법 Point

Point 05 5형식 문장에는 목적격 보어로 명사(구)나 형용사(구)가 올 수 있어요!

- call, name, make 등의 5형식 동사는 목적격 보어로 주로 명사(구)가 온다. 이 경우 목적어와
목적격 보어는 동일한 대상을 가리킨다.
We named the puppy *Brownie*. 우리는 그 강아지를 Brownie라고 이름 지었다. (동격: the puppy = Brownie)
　　　　　목적격 보어(명사)

- find, keep, make 등의 5형식 동사는 목적격 보어로 주로 형용사(구)가 온다. 이 경우 목적어의
상태를 목적격 보어가 보충 설명해 준다.
We thought him *kind*. 우리는 그가 친절하다고 생각했다. (him의 상태: 친절한)
　　　　　목적격 보어(형용사)

Point 06 5형식 문장에서 want, ask, tell, allow, expect, order 등의 동사가 올 경우, 목적격 보어 자리에 to부정사(구)가 와요!

동사 want, ask, tell, allow, expect, order, advise, encourage 등	+	목적어	+	to부정사

(~에게 …하도록 원하다/부탁하다/말하다/허락하다/기대하다/명령하다/조언하다/용기를 북돋우다)

I want you to come with me. 나는 네가 나와 함께 왔으면 한다.

Point 07 5형식 문장에서 서술어가 사역동사이면, 목적격 보어로 동사원형이 주로 와요!

- **사역동사**: '~하게 시키다'라는 뜻의 동사로 make, let, have 등이 있다.

사역동사 make, have, let 등	+	목적어	+	동사원형

(~에게 …을 시키다/~하게 하다/허락하다)

Our teacher made us *clean* the playground. 우리 선생님은 우리가 운동장을 청소하게 했다.
　　　　　　　　목 · 보(동사원형)

- get은 사역동사의 의미(~시키다)를 가지고 있지만, 목적격 보어로 to부정사가 온다.
I got my friend *to help* with work. 나는 친구에게 내 일을 돕도록 시켰다.
　　　　　　목 · 보(to부정사)

- help는 목적격 보어로 동사원형이나 to부정사 둘 다 올 수 있다.
We helped her *(to) do* the dishes. 우리는 그녀가 설거지 하는 것을 도왔다.
　　　　　목 · 보(동사원형 or to부정사)

Point 08 5형식 문장에서 서술어가 지각동사이면, 목적격 보어로 동사원형이나 현재분사(-ing)가 와요!

- **지각동사**: 우리가 감각기관을 통해 보고, 듣고, 느끼는 것을 표현한 동사로, see, look at, watch, hear, listen to, smell, feel 등이 있다.

지각동사 see, look at, watch, hear, listen to, smell, feel 등	+	목적어	+	동사원형 / 현재분사

(~가 …하는 것을 보다/듣다/냄새 맡다/느끼다)

I saw him *cross* the street. 나는 그가 거리를 건너는 것을 보았다.

- 동작이 진행 중임을 강조할 때, 지각동사의 목적격 보어로 현재분사(-ing)를 쓴다.
I saw him *crossing* the street. (현재분사: 진행의 뜻을 강조)
나는 그가 거리를 건너가고 있는 것을 보았다.

핵심만 콕! 문법 Check

A 괄호 안에서 알맞은 말을 고르시오.

1 He had me (hold, holding) his bag.
2 My mom won't let me (go, to go) there.
3 Mr. Kim got me (clean, to clean) the classroom.
4 I felt someone (touch, touched) my shoulder.
5 We saw them (break, to break) the window.
6 Mary and Sam asked me (take, to take) pictures of them.

B 빈칸에 알맞은 말을 〈보기〉에서 골라 알맞은 형태로 쓰시오. (단, 한 번씩만 쓰시오.)

보기			
come	use	give	help

1 I want you _____ me tomorrow.
2 My teacher had me _____ to his office.
3 He will never allow us _____ his computer.
4 The boy expected his parents _____ him a birthday gift.

C 우리말과 뜻이 같도록 어법상 어색한 곳을 고쳐 문장 전체를 다시 쓰시오.

1 She will order them send the packages. (그녀는 그들에게 그 소포를 보내도록 시킬 것이다.)
→ _____

2 Mary asked Tom is quiet in the library. (Mary는 Tom에게 도서관에서 조용히 하라고 부탁했다.)
→ _____

3 I had them to apologize to each other. (나는 그들이 서로 사과하도록 시켰다.)
→ _____

D 우리말과 뜻이 같도록 괄호 안의 말을 바르게 배열하여 문장을 완성하시오.

1 이모는 내게 빨래를 하게 했다. (the laundry, do)
→ My aunt had me _____.

2 그들은 내가 일을 다시 시작하는 것을 도왔다. (to, the, again, me, job, start)
→ They helped _____.

3 그는 내가 그의 이름을 부르는 것을 들었다. (his name, he, call, me, heard)
→ _____.

[1~2] 빈칸에 알맞지 <u>않은</u> 것을 고르시오.

01

> It _____ really great.

① looks
② sounds
③ tastes
④ smells
⑤ touches

02

> Mr. Kim _____ me to study hard for the exam.

① encouraged
② told
③ had
④ asked
⑤ ordered

[3~4] 두 문장의 뜻이 같도록 빈칸에 알맞은 한 단어를 쓰시오.

03 서술형

> We will buy our mom a nice wallet.

→ We will buy a nice wallet _____ our mom.

04 서술형

> The teacher asked me many questions.

→ The teacher asked many questions _____ me.

05 밑줄 친 부분이 어법상 틀린 문장을 고르시오.

① The story <u>sounded boring</u>.
② Her dress <u>looks very lovely</u>.
③ The cookie <u>tastes really well</u>.
④ The leaves will <u>turn red</u> soon.
⑤ She <u>felt angry</u> at the news.

06 우리말과 뜻이 같도록 영어로 나타낼 때 알맞은 것은?

> 그는 가끔 친구들에게 편지를 썼다.

① He often wrote letters for his friends.
② He often wrote letters of his friends.
③ He often wrote letters to his friends.
④ He often wrote his friends letters.
⑤ He often wrote letters his friends.

07 빈칸에 알맞은 말을 고르시오.

> They always kept their room _____.

① cleanly
② darkly
③ dirt
④ messy
⑤ neatly

최다빈출

08 빈칸에 알맞은 말이 나머지 넷과 <u>다른</u> 하나는?

① I will tell the secret _____ you.
② She bought a nice gift _____ me.
③ The English teacher found the book _____ us.
④ My mom cooked delicious food _____ us.
⑤ I am going to make a chocolate cake _____ him.

09 서술형

어법상 잘못된 부분을 찾아 밑줄을 긋고 바르게 고쳐 쓰시오.

> My mom didn't allow us play video games.
> (우리 엄마는 우리가 비디오 게임을 하도록 허락하지 않으셨다.)

_____ → _____

10 빈칸에 알맞지 않은 것은?

> Jenny _____ him to bring more books.

① helped   ② got   ③ wanted
④ had   ⑤ asked

11 빈칸에 공통으로 알맞은 말은?

> • He asked us _____ join the group.
> • Yuna doesn't normally show her feelings _____ her family.

① of   ② to   ③ for
④ in   ⑤ into

12 서술형

우리말과 뜻이 같도록 필요한 단어만 골라 바르게 배열하여 문장을 완성하시오.

> 그는 나에게 그의 컴퓨터를 수리하도록 시켰다.
> (he, made, fix, to, me, his, computer)

→ _____

13 서술형

우리말과 일치하도록 괄호 안의 말을 활용하여 문장을 완성하시오.

> 선생님은 우리에게 절대 지각하지 말라고 말씀하셨다.
> (late, never)

→ Our teacher told us _____
_____ .

14 4형식 문장을 3형식 문장으로 바르게 바꿔 쓴 것을 고르시오.

> They asked me many difficult questions.

① They asked many difficult questions for me.
② They asked many difficult questions to me.
③ They asked many difficult questions of me.
④ They asked me to many difficult questions.
⑤ They asked me of many difficult questions.

15 빈칸에 알맞은 말이 순서대로 바르게 짝지어진 것은?

> A: Hey, the rose over there smells really
>   ⓐ _____ .
> B: Do you think so? I will buy some
>   ⓑ _____ you.

① good, to
② well, to
③ good, for
④ well, for
⑤ good, of

16 우리말을 영어로 옮길 때, 밑줄 친 부분 중 어법상 틀린 것을 고르시오.

우리들 모두는 그가 매우 상냥하다고 생각한다.
→ All of us think him very nicely.
    ①   ②   ③   ④   ⑤

17 밑줄 친 부분의 의미가 〈보기〉와 같은 것은?

┌─ 보기 ┐
The leaves turned red and yellow.
└────────┘

① Can you turn off the radio?
② It's my turn to try.
③ Turn left and you will see it on your right.
④ She turned pale after she heard the news.
⑤ Please turn on the light.

18 서술형

우리말과 뜻이 같도록 괄호 안의 말을 바르게 배열하여 문장을 완성하시오.

우리는 아이들이 요리하는 것을 도왔다.
(the children, we, helped, cook, to)

→ _____

19 서술형

〈보기〉와 같이 두 문장을 한 문장으로 연결하여 다시 쓰시오.

┌─ 보기 ┐
I saw Jenny in the morning. + She was jogging.
→ I saw Jenny jogging in the morning.
└────────┘

I saw Matt an hour ago. + He was talking on the phone.

→ _____

_____

20 빈칸에 공통으로 알맞은 말은?

• I _____ my sister angry.
• My mom _____ me help her clean the house.

① let   ② had   ③ made
④ helped   ⑤ got

21 서술형

〈보기〉와 같이 주어진 말로 시작해 문장을 다시 쓰시오.

┌─ 보기 ┐
I am worried because of the upcoming exam.
→ The upcoming exam makes me worried.
└────────┘

I am happy when listening to music.

→ Listening to music _____

_____.

22 서술형

대화의 흐름이 자연스럽도록 괄호 안의 말을 바르게 배열하여 문장을 완성하시오.

A: Jenny! _____.
   (very, you, happy, look)
   Do you have good news?
B: Yes, I am happy because my father

_____

_____.
   (bought, a, cell phone, new, me)
   Look! Isn't it cool?
A: Wow. It looks great. Was it for your birthday?
B: Yes, it was. It was the best gift ever.

23 서술형

그림과 일치하도록 괄호 안의 말을 활용하여 문장을 완성하시오.

The librarian _____

_____

into the library. (tell)

24 서술형

글의 흐름에 맞게 (A)의 주어진 단어를 바르게 배열하여 문장을
완성하시오.

Minsu visited John's house this afternoon. When he arrived there, John was busy cleaning. Everything near the window was wet because John didn't close the window before he left home and it rained hard in the afternoon. Minsu explained the rainy season in Korea and (A) (the, open, told, to, keep, him, not, window) during this season.

→ _____

_____

25 서술형 심화

다음은 Susie가 마니또에게 받은 짧은 편지글이다. ⓐ～ⓔ 중
어법상 틀린 부분을 두 군데 찾아 해당 문장의 기호를 쓰고, 틀린
부분을 바르게 고쳐 쓰시오.

Dear Susie,

Hi, Susie. I am your Manito, a secret angel. You must be very curious about me. But I cannot ⓐ tell you my name. You know about the rule, right?

I ⓑ want you to laugh more. I like your smile. Your smile ⓒ makes people around you feeling happy. I'll ⓓ give you a present. It's a small thing, but I hope you like it.

I will ⓔ write to you a letter again. Good bye.

Best wishes,
Your secret angel

(1) _____

(2) _____

CHAPTER

02

to부정사

to부정사

동사원형 앞에 **to**를 붙여 만든 것으로, 문장 안에서 명사, 형용사, 또는 부사의 역할을 한다. 주어의 인칭과 수에 따라 형태가 정(定)해지는 것이 아니고(不), 항상 「**to** + 동사원형」형태로 쓴다고 하여 to부정사(不定詞)라고 부른다.

• to부정사의 역할

명사 역할을 하는 to부정사	**English** is fun. To learn English is fun. (주어 역할)
	His plan is **interesting**. His plan is to watch an interesting movie. (보어 역할)
	I want **a hamburger**. I want to have a hamburger. (목적어 역할)
형용사 역할을 하는 to부정사	He has a **fantastic** plan. He has a plan to travel around the world. (명사 수식)
부사 역할을 하는 to부정사	I studied hard. I studied hard to help many people. (동사 수식)

한눈에 쏙! 문법 Chart

명사적 용법	주어 역할 (=가주어 it, 진주어 to부정사)	~하는 것은/이	
	보어 역할	~하는 것	
	목적어 역할	~하는 것을, ~하기를	
	의문사 + to부정사 (=의문사 + 주어 + should + 동사원형)	~할지	
형용사적 용법	~thing/-one/-body + 형용사 + to부정사	~할, ~하는	
	명사 + to부정사구 (=명사 + to부정사 + 전치사)		
부사적 용법	목적 (=in order to + 동사원형, =so as to + 동사원형)	~하기 위해서, ~하러	
	감정의 원인	~해서, ~하니	
	결과	~해서 결국 ~하다/되다	
	판단의 근거	~하다니 (~이 틀림없다)	
의미상의 주어	to부정사의 행위의 주체가 문장의 주어나 목적어와 일치하지 않을 때	to부정사 앞에 for + 목적격	대부분의 경우
		to부정사 앞에 of + 목적격	사람의 성질이나 특성을 나타내는 형용사가 함께 쓰일 때
	to부정사의 행위의 주체가 문장의 주어나 목적어와 같거나, 일반인일 경우	의미상 주어 생략	
형/부 + enough to부정사 = so 형/부 + that + 주어 + can(could) + 동사원형		~할 만큼 충분히 ~하다, 충분히 ~해서 ~할 수 있다	
too + 형/부 + to부정사 = so 형/부 + that + 주어 + can't(couldn't) + 동사원형		너무 ~해서 ~할 수 없다, ~하기에는 너무 ~하다	

핵심만 쏙! 문법 Point

Point 01 to부정사가 문장에서 주어, 보어로 쓰이면, 명사적 용법이에요!

- **to부정사**는 명사처럼 주어, 보어, 목적어 역할을 할 수 있다.
- **주어 역할을 하는 to부정사**: 문장에서 '~하는 것은/이'라고 해석한다.
- 주어로 쓰인 to부정사구가 너무 길면, 대개 가주어 **it**을 주어 자리에 쓰고 to부정사구를 뒤로 보낸다.

  <u>To learn English</u> <u>is</u> <u>difficult</u>. 영어를 배우는 것은 어렵다.
  　　　　주어　　　　동사　　보어

  <u>It</u> <u>is</u> <u>difficult</u> <u>to learn English</u>.
  가주어　　　　　　　　　진주어

  이 때 it을 '가주어', to부정사(구)를 '진주어'라고 부른다.

- **보어 역할을 하는 to부정사**: '~하는 것'이라고 해석한다.
  His job is to teach science. 그의 직업은 과학을 가르치는 것이다.

Point 02 to부정사가 문장에서 목적어로 쓰이면, 명사적 용법이에요!

- **목적어 역할을 하는 to부정사**: '~하는 것을' 또는 '~하기를'이라고 해석된다.
  I want to go on a picnic this weekend. 나는 이번 주말에 소풍 가기를 원한다.

- 목적어로 to부정사만 오는 동사들이 있다.

want, hope, wish, expect, plan, decide, need, promise, learn	+	to부정사

  They decided to study very hard. 그들은 매우 열심히 공부하기로 결심했다.
  I hope to pass the exam. 나는 그 시험에 합격하기를 바란다.

- **to부정사의 부정**: 앞에 'not'이나 'never'를 써 준다.
  I decided not to buy a new bag. 나는 새 가방을 사지 않기로 결심했다.

Point 03 의문사 뒤에 to부정사가 오면 '~할지'로 해석해요!

- 「의문사 + to부정사」는 문장 안에서 주로 동사의 목적어(명사) 역할을 한다.

· who + to부정사: 누구를(에게) ~할지	· what + to부정사: 무엇을 ~할지
· when + to부정사: 언제 ~할지	· how + to부정사: 어떻게 ~할지, ~하는 방법
· where + to부정사: 어디에서 ~할지	· which + to부정사: 어느 것을 ~할지

  I don't know what to do. 나는 무엇을 해야 할지 모른다.
  I don't know how to cook. 나는 요리하는 방법을 모른다.

- 「의문사 + to부정사」는 「의문사 + 주어 + should + 동사원형」으로 바꾸어 쓸 수 있다.
  Please tell me where to stay. → Please tell me where I should stay.
  어디에서 머물러야 할지 제게 말해주세요.

핵심만 콕! 문법 Check

A 괄호 안에서 알맞은 말을 고르시오.

1 (To talk, Talk) with him makes me happy.
2 My dream is (to be, be) an English teacher.
3 He hopes (to see, seeing) her.
4 The man decided (to not send the letter, not to send the letter) to Tom.

B 빈칸에 알맞은 말을 〈보기〉에서 골라 알맞은 형태로 쓰시오.

보기		
pass	study	ask

1 I hope _____ abroad someday.
2 She expects _____ the exam.
3 Bob wants _____ you a question.

C 두 문장의 뜻이 같도록 〈보기〉와 같이 문장을 바꿔 쓰시오.

> 보기
> To exercise regularly is good for you. → It is good for you to exercise regularly.

1 To hang out with friends is fun. → _____
2 To be a famous singer is not easy. → _____

> 보기
> I don't know where to go. → I don't know where I should go.

3 David told me when to leave. → David told me_____.
4 Gloria forgot how to fly the kite.
→ Gloria forgot _____ the kite.

D 우리말과 뜻이 같도록 괄호 안의 말을 활용하여 문장을 완성하시오.

1 Jason은 키가 크기를 원한다. (be, want)
→ Jason _____ _____ _____ tall.

2 무엇을 해야 할지 말해줘. (do)
→ Please tell me _____ _____.

3 그는 어디로 가야 할지 모른다. (go)
→ He doesn't know _____.

4 민준이는 낚시하러 가지 않기로 결심했다. (go fishing, decide)
→ Minjun _____ _____ _____ fishing.

핵심만 쏙! 문법 Point

Point 04 앞의 명사를 꾸미거나 -thing/-one/-body로 끝나는 대명사나 형용사 뒤에서 수식해요! (형용사적 용법)

- to부정사는 앞에 있는 **명사를 꾸며주는 형용사** 역할을 하기도 한다. 이 때, '~할', '~하는'이라고 해석된다.
  Tim has a lot of <u>homework</u> to do. Tim은 해야 할 숙제가 많이 있다.

- -thing/-one/-body로 끝나는 대명사는 형용사가 뒤에서 수식하므로, 「**-thing/-one/-body + 형용사 + to부정사**」순서로 쓴다.
  I want <u>something</u> <u>sweet to eat</u>. 나는 먹을 달콤한 무언가를 원한다.

Point 05 동사와 명사 사이에 전치사가 필요하면 '명사 + to부정사 + 전치사'로 써요! (형용사적 용법)

- to부정사가 수식하는 명사가 전치사의 목적어인 경우, 「**명사 + to부정사 + 전치사**」와 같은 형태로 쓰인다.

  ※ live in a house → a house to live in 살 집
  play with a friend → a friend to play with 함께 놀 친구
  sit on a chair → a chair to sit on 앉을 의자
  write with a pen → a pen to write with 쓸 펜
  write on paper → paper to write on 쓸 종이
  talk to/with someone → someone to talk to/with 이야기할 사람
  cf. to부정사의 동사가 타동사인 경우는 to부정사 뒤에 전치사가 오지 않는다.
  Would you buy me a game to play?
  Would you buy me a game to play with? (X)

  The child needs a friend to play with. 그 아이는 함께 놀 친구가 필요하다.

Point 06 to부정사가 목적을 나타낼 때는 「in order to + 동사원형」 또는 「so as to + 동사원형」으로 바꾸어 쓸 수 있어요! (부사적 용법)

- to부정사가 부사처럼 동사나 형용사, 다른 부사, 또는 문장 전체를 꾸며줄 때 '**to부정사의 부사적 용법**'이라 한다.
  I woke up **early** to finish my homework. 나는 숙제를 끝마치기 위해서 일찍 일어났다.

- **목적을 나타내는 to부정사**: '~하기 위해서', '~하러'라고 해석되며, 「in order to + 동사원형」 또는 「so as to + 동사원형」으로 바꾸어 쓸 수 있다.
  He is in a hurry to arrive on time. 그는 제 시간에 도착하기 위해서 서두르고 있다.
  = He is in a hurry in order to arrive on time.
  = He is in a hurry so as to arrive on time.

Point 07 감정의 원인, 결과, 판단의 근거를 나타내면 부사적 용법이에요!

- **감정의 원인**: 감정을 나타내는 형용사(glad, happy/pleased, sad) 뒤에 to부정사가 오면, '~해서, ~하니'의 뜻이다.
  He was so happy to pass the exam. 그는 그 시험에 합격해서 매우 기뻤다.

- **결과**: 대개 live, grow up, wake up 등의 동사 뒤에 to부정사가 오면, '~해서 결국 …하다/되다'의 뜻이다.
  Justin grew up to be a teacher. Justin은 자라서 선생님이 되었다.

- **판단의 근거**: to부정사가 사람의 성품이나 성질을 나타내는 형용사 뒤에 와서, 판단하는 근거를 설명해 준다.
  Tina must be angry to say so. Tina가 그렇게 말하다니 화가 난 것이 틀림없다.

핵심만 콕! 문법 Check

A 괄호 안에서 알맞은 말을 고르시오.

1 It is time (to go, go) to school.

2 I have (show nothing, nothing to show) you.

3 I need a piece of paper (to write, to write on).

4 He is looking for a new house (to live, to live in).

B 밑줄 친 부분이 부사적 용법 중 어떤 의미로 쓰였는지 쓰시오.

1 He grew up <u>to be</u> a superstar singer. → _____

2 We are glad <u>to see</u> each other again. → _____

3 The man must be rich <u>to buy</u> such an expensive car. → _____

C 〈보기〉를 참고하여, 주어진 두 문장이 같은 뜻이 되도록 빈칸에 알맞은 말을 쓰시오.

> 보기
> He went to the supermarket <u>to buy some milk</u>.
> → He went to the supermarket <u>in order to buy some milk</u>.
> → He went to the supermarket <u>so as to buy some milk</u>.

1 The children ran fast to catch the bus.

→ The children ran fast so _____ _____ _____ the bus.

2 He practiced hard because he wanted to win the race.

→ He practiced hard in _____ _____ _____ the race.

3 Maria studied very hard because she didn't want to fail the exam.

→ Maria studied very hard in _____ _____ _____ the exam.

D 우리말과 뜻이 같도록 괄호 안의 말을 활용하여 문장을 완성하시오.

1 그 노부인은 120살까지 살았다. (live, be)

→ The old lady _____.

2 우리는 마실 것이 필요하다. (drink, something)

→ We need _____.

3 그는 같이 놀 친구가 많다. (play, with)

→ He has many friends _____.

4 그녀는 선생님을 만나기 위해 학교에 왔다. (come, meet)

→ She _____ her teacher.

핵심만 쏙! 문법 Point

Point 08 to부정사의 의미상 주어는 to부정사 앞에 「for + 목적격」으로 써요!

- **to부정사의 의미상의 주어**: to부정사 행위의 주체가 문장의 주어나 목적어와 일치하지 않을 때, to부정사 앞에 의미상의 주어를 쓴다. 대개 「**for + 목적격**」형태로 나타낸다.
  It is easy <u>for him</u> to learn how to ride a bike. 그가 자전거를 타는 법을 배우는 것은 쉬운 일이다.

- 사람의 성질이나 특성을 나타내는 형용사 (nice, kind, smart, wise, silly, polite, rude등)가 함께 오면 to부정사의 의미상의 주어는 「**of + 목적격**」형태로 쓴다.
  It is so nice <u>of you</u> to lend me the book. 그 책을 제게 빌려주다니 당신은 참 친절하군요.

- **to부정사의 의미상의 주어의 생략**: 의미상의 주어가 문장의 주어나 목적어와 같을 경우, 또는 의미상의 주어가 일반적인 사람들 (예: for people, for them, for us 등)일 때에는 생략할 수 있다.
  I decided to study harder. 나는 더 열심히 공부하기로 결심했다. (to study하는사람 = 주어 I)
  It is bad (for people) to tell a lie. (사람들이) 거짓말을 하는 것은 나쁘다. (일반적인 사람)
  I want you to come early. 나는 네가 일찍 오길 원해. (to come하는 사람: 목적어 you)

Point 09 too + 형/부 + to부정사 = so 형/부 that 주어 can't(couldn't)이에요!

- 「**too + 형용사/부사 + to부정사**」: 너무 ~해서 ~할 수 없다, ~하기에는 너무 ~하다
  The boy is too young to understand the question. 그 소년은 그 질문을 이해하기엔 너무 어리다.

- 「**too + 형용사/부사 + to부정사**」는 「**so + 형용사/부사 + that + 주어 + can't + 동사원형**」으로 바꾸어 쓸 수 있다.
  Jaemin was too busy to come to the party. 재민이는 너무 바빠서 파티에 올 수 없었다.
  → Jaemin was so busy that he couldn't come to the party.

Point 10 형/부 enough to부정사 = so 형/부 that 주어 can(could)이에요!

- 「**형용사/부사 + enough + to부정사**」: ~할 만큼 충분히 ~하다, 충분히 ~해서 ~할 수 있다
  The baby is cute enough to enter the contest. 그 아기는 대회에 나갈 수 있을 만큼 충분히 귀엽다.

- 「**형용사/부사 + enough + to부정사**」는 「**so + 형용사/부사 + that + 주어 + can/could**」으로 바꾸어 쓸 수 있다.
  My younger sister is smart enough to solve the problem.
  → My younger sister is so smart that she can solve the problem.
    내 여동생은 그 문제를 해결할 만큼 충분히 똑똑하다.

  He was tall enough to reach the shelf.
  → He was so tall that he could reach the shelf. 그는 선반에 닿을 만큼 충분히 키가 컸다.

핵심만 콕! 문법 Check

A 괄호 안에서 알맞은 말을 고르시오.

1 It was rude (for, of) her to cut in line.
2 There is a magazine (for, of) you to read.
3 Is there any way (for, of) them to study abroad?
4 It was nice (for, of) you to offer your seat to that elderly lady.

B 〈보기〉와 같이 두 문장의 뜻이 통하도록 빈칸에 알맞은 말을 쓰시오.

> **보기**
> The question was <u>too difficult for me to answer</u>.
> → The question was <u>so difficult that I couldn't answer it</u>.

1 He is <u>too weak to carry</u> the boxes.
→ He is _____ the boxes.

2 The girl was <u>too short to reach</u> the book.
→ The girl was _____ the book.

C 〈보기〉와 같이 두 문장의 뜻이 통하도록 빈칸에 알맞은 말을 쓰시오.

> **보기**
> He is <u>old enough to drive</u> a car.
> → He is <u>so old that he can drive</u> a car.

1 I am <u>strong enough to lift</u> the heavy box.
→ I am _____ the heavy box.

2 The man was <u>rich enough to</u> buy the house.
→ The man was _____ the house.

D 우리말과 뜻이 같도록 괄호 안의 말을 활용하여 문장을 완성하시오.

1 이 셔츠는 너무 커서 나는 그것을 입을 수가 없다. (so, that, can't)
→ This shirt is _____ it.

2 그 질문에 대답하는 것은 그녀에게는 어렵다. (answer)
→ It is very difficult _____ the question.

3 그 수프는 너무 뜨거워서 먹을 수 없다. (too, to)
→ The soup is _____.

4 그는 달리기 시합에서 이길 만큼 충분히 빠르다. (fast)
→ He is _____ win the race.

[1~2] 밑줄 친 it의 쓰임이 나머지와 다른 하나를 고르시오.

01

① It is easy to open the door.
② It was the present for children.
③ It was difficult to win the game.
④ It is possible to attend the meeting.
⑤ It isn't easy to work out every day.

02

① It's good to take vitamin C.
② To me, it's the best pen in the world.
③ It will be exciting to learn to snowboard.
④ I think that it is important to listen to parents.
⑤ Isn't it difficult to wake up early in the morning?

03 서술형

빈칸에 공통으로 알맞은 전치사를 쓰시오.

> • Give me a pencil to write _____.
> • He is looking for a roommate to live _____.

→ _____

04 빈칸에 가장 알맞은 것은?

> G: What's wrong?
> B: I don't know _____ to get to the post office.
> G: Why don't you look at the map?
> B: That's a good idea.

① why   ② what   ③ who
④ how   ⑤ when

05 서술형

우리말과 일치하도록 빈칸에 알맞은 말을 쓰시오.

> Tom은 너무 놀라서 움직일 수 없었다.

→ Tom was _____ _____
_____ _____ .

06 최다빈출

밑줄 친 부분의 쓰임이 〈보기〉와 같은 것은?

> 보기
> I'm happy to see you again.

① Ivan grew up to be an actor.
② David is glad to be the winner.
③ Terra woke up to finish her homework.
④ She can't be poor to buy that sports car.
⑤ This lake must be dangerous to swim in.

07 서술형

두 문장의 뜻이 같도록 괄호 안의 단어를 사용하여 문장을 완성하시오. (부정은 축약형으로 쓰시오)

> (1) The girl is too young to get her driver's license. (so, that)

= The girl is _____ young _____
_____ _____ get her driver's license.

> (2) He cooks well enough to be a chef. (so, that)

= He cooks _____ well _____
_____ _____ be a chef.

08

나는 쓸 수 있는 종이가 좀 필요해.

① I need some paper to write.
② I need to write some paper on.
③ I need some paper to write on.
④ I need to write some paper on.
⑤ I need some paper to write with.

09

그 아이들은 함께 할 게임을 원해.

① They want a game play together.
② They want a game to play together.
③ They want a game play with together.
④ They want a game to play with together.
⑤ They want a game to play in together.

10 밑줄 친 부분이 어법상 옳은 것은?

① It is dangerous of him drive fast.
② It is necessary of her to study hard.
③ It was kind of him to help the poor.
④ It was polite for her to greet the neighbors.
⑤ It is important for he to work out regularly.

11 밑줄 친 부분이 어법상 틀린 것은?

① Sora is happy to see you.
② Bora wants something to eat hot.
③ Sangjun needs a friend to talk to.
④ Sangmin doesn't know where to go.
⑤ Jimin bought a soccer ball to play with.

12 서술형

밑줄 친 단어 tips가 무엇에 관한 것인지 본문에서 찾아 쓰시오.

G: Could you tell me how to save money wisely?
B: Why not? Here are some tips.

→ _____

13 괄호 안의 단어를 어법에 맞게 바꾸어 쓸 때, 순서대로 알맞게 짝지어진 것은?

• You'd better use three banks ⓐ (control) your money.
• Shop around where you can get the best price for things you want ⓑ (buy).

① to control, to buy ② controlled, to buy
③ to control, buying ④ controlling, to buy
⑤ controlling, buying

14 서술형

우리말과 같은 뜻이 되도록 괄호 안의 말을 바르게 배열하여 문장을 완성하시오.

Sally는 바나나를 조금 사기 위해서 슈퍼마켓에 갔다.
(to, bananas, buy, some)

→ Sally went to the supermarket _____
_____ .

15 빈칸에 알맞은 말은?

He has to write a letter. But _____
_____ . He needs a pen.

① he has someone to help.
② he has nothing to write on.
③ he has nothing to write with.
④ he has something to work on.
⑤ he has some friends to play with.

16 밑줄 친 부분의 쓰임이 〈보기〉와 같은 것을 모두 고르면? (2개)

> **보기**
> Let's do a simple experiment to see what volcanoes are.

① To see is to believe.
② He wants to ride a taxi.
③ My hobby is to read books.
④ I bought a camera to take pictures.
⑤ I didn't ring the bell not to wake the children.

17 서술형

〈보기〉에서 알맞은 말을 골라 문장을 완성하시오.
(단, 각 단어는 한 번씩만 사용)

> **보기**
> a   pen   something   to
> warm   wear   with   write

(1) Sue feels really cold now. She wants
_____ _____ _____
_____.

(2) Tom lost his pen. He will buy _____
_____ to _____ _____.

18 서술형

우리말과 같은 뜻이 되도록 주어진 단어를 바르게 배열하여 문장을 완성하시오.

> 버스에서 큰소리로 통화하는 것은 무례하다.
> (rude, talk, on the phone, is, to, it, loudly)

→ _____
_____ on the bus.

19 밑줄 친 (A)와 같은 용법으로 쓰인 것을 모두 고르면? (2개)

> I haven't been to Hong Kong. I heard that there are many interesting things (A) to do. I am very excited. I hope the weather will be nice.

① She has many socks to wash.
② He is in a hurry to get a seat.
③ I don't know when to meet her.
④ It is difficult to learn new languages.
⑤ The professor gave his students a difficult project to do.

최다빈출

20 다음 글의 ⓐ to cheer와 그 쓰임이 같은 것은?

> I am glad that Mr. Park became my homeroom teacher again. He is one of the best teachers in my school. His humor has the ability ⓐ to cheer us up when we are depressed.

① It is hard to learn French.
② I hope to learn Spanish this year.
③ I want to have a sense of humor like Mr. Park's.
④ I am very happy to help others with my talent.
⑤ Today all students wrote down one thing to achieve next year.

21 서술형

주어진 문장을 to부정사를 사용하여 〈보기〉와 같이 한 문장으로 만드시오.

┌─ 보기 ┌─────────────────────────┐
I woke up early this morning. I made breakfast.
→ I woke up early to make breakfast this morning.
└──────────────────────────────────┘

Daniel went to the hospital. He needed to see a doctor.

→ _____

_____

22 서술형

다음 표를 보고 〈보기〉를 참고 하여 괄호 안의 단어를 사용하여 Jane과 Kevin에 관한 문장을 완성하시오. (단, 현재 시제로 쓸 것)

Who	What	Why
Tina	wash the dishes	help her mother
Jane	study hard	pass the exam
Kevin	exercise every day	stay fit

┌─ 보기 ┌─────────────────────────┐
Tina <u>washes the dishes to help her mother</u>. (to)
└──────────────────────────────────┘

→ (1) Jane _____

_____. (so as to)

→ (2) Kevin _____

_____. (in order to)

[23~24] 다음 글을 읽고 물음에 답하시오.

Tomorrow is my best friend's birthday, but (A) <u>나는 너무 바빠서 쇼핑을 갈 수가 없었다</u> for his birthday present. After school, I was thinking about his present, and then I had a bright idea. I asked our friends to say something ⓐ <u>make</u> him laugh and recorded them.

23 밑줄 친 (A)를 영어로 바르게 옮긴 것은?

① I was busy enough to go shopping
② I was not enough busy to go shopping
③ I was too busy that I could go shopping
④ I was so busy that I couldn't go shopping
⑤ I was not busy, so that I could go shopping

24 밑줄 친 ⓐ를 어법에 맞게 고친 것은?

① making   ② to make   ③ make to
④ made   ⑤ makes

25 서술형 심화

다음 그림을 보고 〈보기〉와 같이 주어진 단어를 사용하여 문장을 완성하시오.

┌─ 보기 ┌─────────────────────────┐

Two years ago, I was <u>too short to ride the roller coaster</u>, but I'm <u>tall enough to ride it</u> now. (short, tall, ride)
└──────────────────────────────────┘

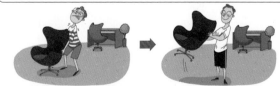

→ A year ago, my brother _____

_____, but he _____

_____ now. (weak, strong, lift)

CHAPTER
03

동명사

동명사

「동사원형 + ing」의 형태로, 동사의 성질을 가진 채로 문장 안에서 명사처럼 주어, 보어, 목적어의 역할을 한다. 동명사가 목적어의 역할을 할 때, 동사에 따라 동명사만을 목적어로 취하는 경우가 있다. 반면에 to부정사만을 목적어로 취하는 동사도 있으므로 주의해야 한다.

한눈에 쏙! 문법 Chart

동명사의 역할	주어와 보어로 쓰일 때는 to부정사와 바꾸어 쓸 수 있다. Learning (=To learn) a foreign language is useful. His dream is working (=to work) for the UN. Everyone enjoyed participating (=to participate) in the festival. 목적어로 쓰인 경우는 to부정사로 바꿀 수 없다. Are you interested in playing baseball? (playing ≠ to play) Did you enjoy watching the movie? (watching ≠ to watch)
동명사를 목적어로 취하는 동사들	mind, enjoy, give up, avoid, finish, escape, practice, stop → megafeps(메가펩스)
to부정사만을 목적어로 취하는 동사들	want, expect, hope, wish, decide, plan, promise, refuse 등
동명사와 to부정사를 의미차이 없이 목적어로 취하는 동사들	start, begin, like, love, hate, continue
동명사와 to부정사를 목적어로 취할 때 뜻이 달라지는 동사들	remember + ⌈ 동명사(-ing): (과거) ~했던 것을 기억하다 ⌊ to부정사: (미래) ~할 것을 기억하다 forget + ⌈ 동명사(-ing): (과거) ~했던 것을 잊다 ⌊ to부정사: (미래) ~할 것을 잊다 try + ⌈ 동명사(-ing): (시도) 시험 삼아 ~해 보다 ⌊ to부정사: (노력) ~하려고 애쓰다 stop + ⌈ 동명사(-ing): ~하는 것을 멈추다 ⌊ to부정사: ~하기 위해 멈추다(부사적용법)
동명사의 의미상 주어	동명사 앞에 소유격이나 목적격으로 나타낸다.

Point 01 동명사(-ing)는 문장에서 명사처럼 주어, 보어, 목적어로 쓰여요!

- **동명사의 형태와 역할:** 동명사는 「**동사원형 + ing**」의 형태로, 문장에서 명사처럼 **주어, 보어, 목적어**의 역할을 한다.
  - **주어로 쓰이는 경우**는 '~하는 것(은/이)'로 해석된다. 이 때 **동명사는 대개 단수 취급**한다.
    Learning English is fun. 영어를 배우는 것은 재미있다.
  - **보어로 쓰이는 경우**는 '~하는 것(이다)'로 해석된다.
    My favorite activity is reading novels. 내가 가장 좋아하는 활동은 소설을 읽는 것이다.
- **주어나 보어로 쓰인 동명사**는 to부정사와 바꾸어 쓸 수 있다.
  Eating (=To eat) breakfast is good for you. 아침을 먹는 것은 너에게 좋다.
  His dream is traveling (=to travel) around the world. 그의 꿈은 세계를 여행하는 것이다.

Point 02 동명사만을 목적어로 취하는 동사들은 megafeps(메가팹스)로 외워요!

- **동사의 목적어로 쓰이는 동명사:** mind, enjoy, give up, avoid, finish, escape, practice, stop 등의 동사는 동명사를 목적어로 취한다.
  Yumi enjoys going to the movies. 유미는 영화 보러 가는 것을 즐긴다.
  When could you finish making the robot? 너는 로봇 만드는 것을 언제 끝낼 수 있을 것 같니?
  cf. stop 뒤에 오는 to부정사는 목적을 뜻하는 부사적용법이다.
    People stopped to see what happened. 사람들은 무슨 일인 지 보기 위해 멈췄다.
- **전치사의 목적어로 쓰이는 동명사:** 전치사의 목적어로 동사가 올 때에는 반드시 동명사 형태로 온다.
  We can't learn anything without making mistakes. 우리는 실수하지 않고 무언가를 배울 수 없다.
  Ann is interested in teaching children. Ann은 아이들을 가르치는 것에 관심이 있다.

Point 03 동명사의 의미상 주어는 동명사 앞에 소유격이나 목적격으로 쓰여요!

- **동명사의 의미상의 주어:** 동명사의 행위자가 문장의 주어나 목적어, 혹은 일반인일 때는 의미상 주어를 따로 쓰지 않지만, 그 이외의 경우에는 동명사 앞에 소유격이나 목적격으로 의미상의 주어를 나타낸다.
  I love listening to music when cleaning my room. (주어가 동명사의 행위자)
  나는 내 방을 청소할 때 음악 듣는 것을 좋아한다.
  Thank you for helping me move the desk. (목적어가 동명사의 행위자) 책상을 옮기는 것을 도와줘서 고마워.
  Smoking is bad for you. (동명사의 행위자가 일반인) 흡연은 건강에 나쁘다.
  Do you mind my/me joining your club? 너는 내가 너희 동아리에 가입하는 것을 꺼리니?
- **동명사의 부정:** 「not/never + 동명사」의 형태로 쓴다.
  Never giving up a challenge is his motto. 도전을 결코 포기하지 않는 것이 그의 좌우명이다.

핵심만 콕! 문법 Check

A 괄호 안에서 알맞은 말을 모두 고르시오.

1 My dream is (become, becoming) a scientist.

2 (Make, Making, To make) a model airplane is exciting.

3 His dream for the future is (help, helping, to help) poor people.

4 My parents don't like (I, my, me) wanting to become a pro-gamer.

B 빈칸에 알맞은 말을 〈보기〉에서 골라 알맞은 형태로 쓰시오.

보기	play	go	paint	run

1 학생들은 캠핑 가는 것에 대해 이야기하고 있었다.

→ Students were talking about _____ camping.

2 그들은 벽에 페인트 칠하는 것을 곧 끝낼 것이다.

→ They will finish _____ the wall soon.

3 지수는 체육대회에 나가기 위해 달리기를 매일 연습하고 있다.

→ Jisu practices _____ every day to enter the Sports Festival.

4 기호는 컴퓨터 게임을 하는 것을 그만두기로 결심했다.

→ Giho decided to stop _____ computer games.

C 우리말과 뜻이 같도록 괄호 안의 말을 바르게 배열하여 문장을 완성하시오.

1 나의 목표는 매일 아침 일찍 일어나는 것이다. (is, waking up early, my goal)

→ _____ every morning.

2 배드민턴을 치는 것이 내 여동생의 가장 좋아하는 여가 활동이다. (is, badminton, playing)

→ _____ my sister's favorite leisure activity.

3 친구들과 자전거를 타는 것은 재미있다. (is, with friends, riding a bike)

→ _____ fun.

4 그의 계획은 학교 말하기대회에서 우승하는 것이다. (the school speech contest, winning, is)

→ His plan _____.

D 우리말과 뜻이 같도록 괄호 안의 말을 활용하여 문장을 완성하시오.

1 그는 약속에 늦지 않는 것이 중요하다고 생각한다. (be)

→ He thinks that _____ _____ late for an appointment is important.

2 제가 옆자리에 앉아도 될까요? (sit, mind)

→ Would you _____ _____ _____ next to you?

3 Peter는 로봇 만들기에 관심이 많다. (make, in, interested)

→ Peter is very _____ _____ a robot.

4 그들은 학교 마당 세일을 열 것을 바란다. (have, wish)

→ They _____ _____ a school yard sale.

핵심만 쏙! 문법 Point

Point 04 미래지향동사는 to부정사를, megafeps는 동명사를 목적어로 취해요!

■ 동명사만을 목적어로 취하는 동사

> mind, enjoy, give up, avoid, finish, escape, practice, stop 등

They just finished painting the wall. 그들은 막 벽을 칠하는 것을 끝냈다.
She should stop spending so much time on the Internet.
그녀는 인터넷에 너무 많은 시간을 쓰는 것을 멈춰야 한다.

■ to부정사만을 목적어로 취하는 동사 (미래지향동사)

> want, expect, hope, wish, decide, plan, promise, refuse 등

He hoped to climb Mt. Everest someday. 그는 언젠가 에베레스트 산을 등반하기를 희망했다.
He promised to take me on the trip. 그는 그 여행에 나를 데려갈 것을 약속했다.

Point 05 동명사와 to부정사를 모두 목적어로 취하는 동사들도 있어요!

■ 동명사와 to부정사 둘 다 목적어로 올 수 있는 동사들이 있다.

- 의미상 차이가 없는 경우: start, begin, like, love, hate, continue 등의 동사는 의미 차이 없이
to부정사와 동명사를 모두 목적어로 취할 수 있다.
She likes to make friends with new people. 그녀는 새로운 사람들과 친구가 되는 것을 좋아한다.
= She likes making friends with new people.

- 의미상 차이가 있는 경우: remember, forget, try 등의 동사

remember + 동명사(-ing)	(과거) ~했던 것을 기억하다	I remembered seeing her there. 나는 그녀를 거기서 본 걸 기억해.
remember + to부정사	(미래) ~할 것을 기억하다	She remembered to leave her bag at home. 그녀는 가방을 집에 두고 와야 한다는 것을 기억했다.
forget + 동명사(-ing)	(과거) ~했던 것을 잊다	She forgot leaving her bag at home. 그녀는 가방을 집에 두고 온 것을 잊었다.
forget + to부정사	(미래) ~할 것을 잊다	Don't forget to lock the door. 문 잠그는 것을 잊지마.
try + 동명사(-ing)	(시도) 시험 삼아 ~해 보다	He tried pressing the button. 그는 버튼을 시험 삼아 눌러 보았다.
try + to부정사	(노력) ~하려고 애쓰다	They tried to open the door. 그들은 문을 열려고 애썼다.

Point 06 자주 나오는 동명사 표현은 외워요!

■ 자주 쓰이는 동명사 표현은 다음과 같다.

go ~ing	~하러 가다	look forward to ~ing	~할 것을 고대하다
feel like ~ing	~하고 싶다	How/What about ~ing?	~하는 게 어때?
spend 시간/돈 (in/on) ~ing	~하는 데 시간/돈을 쓰다	waste 시간/돈 (in/on) ~ing	~하는 데 시간/돈을 낭비하다
be good at ~ing	~을 잘하다	be used to ~ing	~하는 데 익숙하다
keep ~ing	계속 ~하다	cf. used to + 동사원형	예전에 ~ 했었다 (지금은 아니다)

핵심만 콕! 문법 Check

A 괄호 안에서 알맞은 말을 고르시오.

1 My school goes (camp, camping) from Wednesday to Friday.
2 He is good at (fix, fixing) things like bikes and cars.
3 Mom is used to (get up, getting up) early in the morning.
4 I used (live, to live, to living) in London. Now I live in Seoul.
5 How about (visit, visiting) the history museum tomorrow?
6 George spent his money (buy, buying) nice shoes.
7 We are looking forward to (go, going) on our field trip.

B 다음 괄호 안에 주어진 동사를 알맞은 형태로 바꾸어 빈칸에 쓰시오.

1 Minsu hopes _____ the school writing competition. (win)
2 He finished _____ his report. (write)
3 Mingming expects _____ Korea next month. (visit)
4 Sujin practices _____ to enter a contest. (sing)
5 I plan _____ around the world someday. (travel)
6 Do you mind _____ the door? (close)
7 My father wants _____ a new car. (buy)

C 우리말과 뜻이 같도록 〈보기〉에서 알맞은 단어를 골라 빈칸을 완성하시오.

보기					
catch	avoid	exercise	pick	meet	watch
waste	stop	give up	give	decide	forget

1 우리는 물을 낭비하는 것을 멈춰야 한다.
→ We should _____ water.

2 그는 첫 차를 타는 것을 포기했다.
→ He _____ the first train.

3 나는 오늘부터 매일 운동하기로 결심했다.
→ I _____ every day from now on.

4 Sally는 Tom과 학교에서 우연히 마주치는 것을 피했다.
→ Sally _____ Tom by chance at school.

5 그는 거리에 있는 쓰레기를 줍기 위해 멈췄다.
→ He _____ up some trash on the street.

6 그녀는 그녀의 아들에게 열쇠를 주었다는 것을 잊어버렸다.
→ She _____ her key to her son.

7 TV 보면서 시간을 낭비하지 마라.
→ Don't _____ time _____ TV.

내신 만점! 실전 기출

[1~3] 빈칸에 알맞은 것을 고르시오.

01

_____ a speech contest is my goal this year.

① Win   ② To winning   ③ Winning
④ Won   ⑤ Wins

02

He hopes _____ around the world someday.

① to travel   ② traveling   ③ traveled
④ travels   ⑤ to traveling

03

My teacher gave me some tips on _____ English.

① study   ② studying   ③ to study
④ studies   ⑤ to studying

04 어법상 어색한 곳을 찾아 바르게 고쳐 쓰시오.

Mandy didn't feel like to go out at night.

_____ → _____

[5~6] 빈칸에 알맞지 않은 말을 고르시오.

05

She _____ to get up early in the morning.

① wanted   ② planned   ③ promised
④ decided   ⑤ avoided

06

He _____ taking pictures at the park.

① finished   ② enjoyed   ③ practiced
④ hoped   ⑤ gave up

07 〈보기〉에서 알맞은 말을 골라 우리말과 뜻이 같도록 문장을 배열할 때 첫 번째 빈칸에 올 단어는?

┌─ 보기 ─────────────────────────┐
(friends, to, is, nice, important, being)
나는 친구들에게 친절한 것이 중요하다고 생각한다.
→ I think _____ _____ _____
_____ _____ _____.
└────────────────────────────────┘

① friends   ② nice   ③ being
④ important   ⑤ is

[8~9] 우리말과 뜻이 같도록 괄호 안의 단어를 빈칸에 알맞은 형태로 쓰시오.

08 서술형

그는 벽에 그림을 달려고 애썼다. (hang)

→ He tried _____ a picture on the wall.

09 서술형

나는 밤에 늦게까지 자지 않는 것에 익숙하다. (stay up)

→ I am used to _____ late at night.

[10~11] 짝지어진 대화가 <u>어색한</u> 것을 고르시오.

10

① A: Did you call your mom?

   B: No, I forgot to call her.

② A: Shhh! The baby is sleeping.

   B: OK. I will stop to play the piano.

③ A: This computer doesn't work fast.

   B: What about getting a new one?

④ A: What are you doing?

   B: I am trying to find my lost contact lens.

⑤ A: Hey, don't you remember meeting me at the party?

   B: Yes, I remember you!

11

① A: What kind of movies do you like?

   B: I like to watch romance movies.

② A: Where did Jiho and Mina go?

   B: They went shopping to buy some snacks.

③ A: This door doesn't open.

   B: Try to press the red button. It might work.

④ A: You know our school festival is coming.

   B: Yeah. I am really looking forward to seeing it.

⑤ A: What did you do last weekend?

   B: I spent the whole weekend taking care of my sister.

12 서술형

우리말과 뜻이 같도록 괄호 안의 말을 활용하여 영작하시오. (5단어)

영화를 보는 게 어때? (what, watch a movie)

→ _____ ?

최다빈출

13 어법상 옳은 문장은?

① My hobby is play the violin.

② He finished do his homework.

③ I enjoy read a book every day.

④ How about climb Mt. Seorak next weekend?

⑤ Susie is interested in entering a dance contest.

최다빈출

[14~15] 어법상 <u>어색한</u> 것을 고르시오.

14

① Amy likes dancing to music.

② I don't feel like to go out today.

③ Frank doesn't mind lending his car to his brother.

④ She decided to keep a diary every day.

⑤ Brian planned to clean his room every day.

15

① Eating vegetables is good for you.

② Many people think that seeing is believing.

③ Bill wants to travel around the world by bike.

④ They stopped playing the game because of rain.

⑤ Janet was not used to get up early in the morning.

16 서술형

〈보기〉와 같이 주어진 문장을 바꾸어 쓸 때 빈칸에 알맞은 말을 쓰시오.

┌─ 보기 ──────────────────────┐
Ryan lent some money to Tom. He remembers it.

→ Ryan remembers lending some money to Tom.
└────────────────────────────┘

(1) Sally bought some apples the other day. She remembers it.

→ Sally _____
some apples the other day.

(2) Mom told me to water the garden. I forgot it.

→ I _____ the garden.

17 빈칸 ⓐ∼ⓒ에 들어갈 말을 순서대로 바르게 나열한 것은?

My goal for this year is ⓐ _____ computer games too much. I will also try ⓑ _____ my room clean. After I finish ⓒ _____ something, I will put it back in its place.

① playing not, to keep, to use
② not playing, to keep, using
③ playing not, keeping, using
④ not playing, keeping, to use
⑤ not playing, keeping, using

18 ⓐ∼ⓔ중 어법상 틀린 것은?

Let me introduce my family. My father works for a bank. He likes ⓐ playing tennis. My mother is a housewife. She enjoys ⓑ cooking. My sister is a student. Her hobby is ⓒ take pictures. I am interested in ⓓ playing the violin. I hope ⓔ to be a music teacher in the future.

① ⓐ　　② ⓑ　　③ ⓒ　　④ ⓓ　　⑤ ⓔ

19 〈보기〉에서 어법상 옳은 문장은 모두 몇 개인가?

┌─ 보기 ──────────────────────┐
ⓐ Did you finish to wash the dishes?
ⓑ Did you enjoy my playing the violin?
ⓒ I will never give up climbing Mt. Everest!
ⓓ Getting up early in the morning is a good habit.
ⓔ Brenda practices to sing and dance for her school talent show.
└────────────────────────────┘

① 1개　　② 2개　　③ 3개　　④ 4개　　⑤ 5개

20 ⓐ∼ⓔ의 우리말 해석이 어색한 것은?

March 20th

I ⓐ forgot to set my alarm clock last night, so I got up late. After ⓑ washing myself, I hurried to school. On the way, I saw something on the street, and I ⓒ stopped to pick it up. It was a wallet with a student ID card inside. I ⓓ remembered hearing about the Lost and Found at my school. During lunch time, I went there to report the wallet. Later, the owner called to thank me. I ⓔ felt proud of being honest.

① ⓐ: 설정한 것을 잊었다
② ⓑ: 세면하기
③ ⓒ: 그것을 줍기 위해 멈췄다
④ ⓓ: 들었던 것을 기억했다
⑤ ⓔ: 정직했던 것에 대해 자랑스러웠다

21 밑줄 친 ⓐ~ⓔ 중 어법상 옳지 <u>않은</u> 것을 <u>모두</u> 고른 것은?

> Dear Paulo,
>
> Thank you for ⓐ <u>send</u> me a letter. I learned more about you from it. You told me you like ⓑ <u>to read</u> mystery books, and I do, too. I also love ⓒ <u>reading</u> comic books. When you come to Korea, we can spend some time ⓓ <u>to visit</u> famous places in Seoul together! I look forward ⓔ <u>to see</u> you soon!

① ⓐ, ⓒ, ⓔ   ② ⓑ, ⓒ, ⓓ   ③ ⓐ, ⓓ, ⓔ
④ ⓐ, ⓑ, ⓓ   ⑤ ⓑ, ⓓ, ⓔ

22 서술형

우리말과 뜻이 같도록 괄호 안의 단어를 활용하여 문장을 완성하시오. (필요하면 단어의 형태를 바꾸고, 동명사를 주어로 하여 문장을 만드시오.)

> Mom: Tony, it's already 9 o'clock. Wake up!
> Tony: But it's Saturday today. I don't have to wake up early.
> Mom: Tony, _____.
> (규칙적으로 일어나는 것이 중요하다.)
> Tony: All right, Mom.

→ _____

(important, getting, is, up, regularly)

23 서술형

다음 우리말과 뜻이 같도록 조건에 맞춰 〈보기〉에서 필요한 단어들을 골라 한 문장으로 쓰시오.

> **조건**
> 1. 필요하면 단어의 어형 변형 가능함.
> 2. 다른 단어를 추가할 수 없음.

> **보기**
> pleasure, thank you, of, taking, for, lost puppy, me, help, my, finding

제 잃어버린 강아지를 찾는 것을 도와 주셔서 감사합니다.

→ _____

24 서술형

다음 세 가지 조건에 따라 문장을 완성하시오.

> **조건**
> 1. 동명사 사용
> 2. 괄호 안의 말을 모두 활용하되 필요하면 형태를 바꾸시오.
> 3. 우리말 뜻: 너는 넘어지지 않고 자전거 타기를 배울 수 없다.

→ You can't learn _____
_____

(without, fall, ride a bike)

25 서술형 심화

대화의 흐름이 자연스럽도록 괄호 안의 말을 활용하여 문장을 완성하시오.

> A : The talent show will start soon.
> B : That's right. What are you going to do?
> A : I think I (1) _____.
>   (good, do voices) I'm going to do voices of celebrities.
> B : Really? (2) _____.
>   (look forward, hear)

(1) _____

(2) _____

CHAPTER
04

분사

분사

동사가 형용사처럼 명사를 꾸미거나 보어의 역할을 하고 싶을 때 동사원형에 -ing를 붙이거나 -ed를 붙인 형태로
그 모습을 바꾼 것을 '분사'라고 한다. 동사원형에 -ing가 붙은 것은 현재분사로 능동, 진행의 의미를 나타내고,
동사원형에 -ed를 붙인 것은 과거분사로 수동과 완료의 의미를 나타낸다.

한눈에 쏙! 문법 Chart

• 분사

현재분사(-ing)	능동, 진행의 의미	The singing girl is my friend. playing
과거분사(p.p)	수동, 완료의 의미	You should clean up broken glass.
분사구문 만드는 법	① 접속사 생략 ② 주어가 같으면 생략 (다르면 남겨 둔다) ③ 동사를 「동사원형+ing」로 바꿈	As she listened to music, she took a walk. → Listening to music, she took a walk.

핵심만 쏙! 문법 Point

Point 01 현재분사는 능동이나 진행의 의미를 나타내요!

- **현재분사의 형태와 역할**: 현재분사는 「동사원형-ing」의 형태이다. 문장에서 형용사처럼 명사를 수식하거나 보어 역할을 한다.

- **현재분사의 의미**: 현재분사는 **능동**(~하는)이나 **진행**(~하고 있는)의 의미를 담고 있다.
  A rolling stone gathers no moss. 구르는 돌은 이끼가 끼지 않는다. (능동)
  The baby is crying. 그 아기가 울고 있다. (진행)

  ※ 현재분사가 수식어구와 함께 올 때는 뒤에서 수식한다.
  The girl waiting for me outside is my younger sister. 밖에서 나를 기다리는 그 소녀가 내 여동생이다.

Point 02 과거분사는 수동이나 완료의 의미를 나타내요!

- **과거분사**의 형태와 쓰임: 과거분사는 대개 「동사원형-ed」의 형태이다. 문장에서 형용사처럼 쓰인다.

- **과거분사의 의미**: 과거분사는 **수동**(~된)과 **완료**(~한)의 의미를 나타낸다.
  This product is made in Korea. 이 제품은 한국에서 만들어졌다. (수동)
  There are a lot of fallen leaves on the street. 거리에 낙엽이 많이 있다. (완료)

Point 03 감정 유발의 원인을 나타낼 때는 현재분사(-ing), 감정을 느끼는 주체일 때는 과거분사(-ed)를 써요!

현재분사 (감정 유발의 원인)	과거분사 (감정을 느끼는 주체)
interesting 재미있는	interested 관심이 있는
boring 지겨운	bored 지루한
exciting 흥미로운	excited 흥분한, 신난
confusing 혼란스럽게 하는	confused 혼란스러워 하는
satisfying 만족스러운	satisfied 만족한
disappointing 실망시키는	disappointed 실망한
surprising 놀라운	surprised 놀란

The class was very boring. 그 수업은 무척 지겨웠다.
He felt bored in the class. 그는 수업에 지루함을 느꼈다.

핵심만 콕! 문법 Check

A 우리말과 뜻이 같도록 괄호 안에서 알맞은 말을 고르시오.

1 우리는 새들이 노래하는 소리를 들을 수 있었다.

→ We could hear the birds (sung, singing).

2 벤치에 앉아 있는 여자아이들은 이야기를 하고 있다.

→ The girls (sat, sitting) on the bench are having chat.

3 그 건물은 작년에 지어졌다.

→ The building was (building, built) last year.

B 밑줄 친 부분을 어법에 맞게 고쳐 쓰시오.

1 This is the picture <u>painting</u> by my friend.   → _____

2 The window was <u>breaking</u> by the strong wind. → _____

3 The food <u>cook</u> by my mom tastes delicious. → _____

4 We have a cat <u>calling</u> Coco.   → _____

C 〈보기〉에서 알맞은 동사를 골라 분사의 형태로 바꾸어 빈칸에 쓰시오.

보기			
amaze	use	bark	excite

1 I don't like dogs _____ at people.

(나는 사람을 향해 짖는 개를 좋아하지 않는다.)

2 He told us an _____ story. (그는 우리에게 놀라운 이야기를 해 주었다.)

3 He was thinking about buying a(n) _____ car.

(그는 중고차를 사는 것에 대해 생각하고 있었다.)

D 괄호 안에 주어진 단어를 분사의 형태로 바꾸어 빈칸에 쓰시오.

1 The movie was great. All of us really liked it. (satisfy)

→ The movie was very _____.

→ We were _____ with the movie.

2 Jimmy was so young and healthy. People never expected his death. (shock)

→ Jimmy's death was so _____.

→ People were _____ at Jimmy's death.

핵심만 쏙! 문법 Point

Point 04 현재분사는 형용사의 역할, 동명사는 명사의 역할을 해요!

- **현재분사**는 형용사처럼 명사를 수식하거나 보어로 쓰여 명사의 상태를 설명한다. 또, be동사와 함께 진행형으로 쓰이기도 한다.

구분	역할	예문
현재분사	명사 수식 (상태)	A crying child is difficult to control. (우는 아이)
	보어	We heard her singing beautifully. (아름답게 노래하는)
	진행형	My sister is making cookies. (쿠키를 만들고 있다)

- **동명사**는 명사처럼 주어, 목적어, 보어, 전치사의 목적어 역할을 하거나 명사 앞에 쓰여 그 명사의 용도를 나타내기도 한다.

구분	역할	예문
동명사	주어	Reading novels is interesting. (소설을 읽는 것)
	보어	Her hobby is collecting coins. (동전을 모으는 것)
	목적어	Our family likes eating out. (나가서 먹는 것)
	전치사의 목적어	He is good at singing. (노래하는 것)
	명사의 용도(목적)	We should bring a sleeping bag. (침낭)

Point 05 분사구문을 만들 때는 접(속사 생략) + 주(어생략) + 동(사+ing)이에요!

- **분사구문을 만드는 법**
  ① 부사절의 접속사를 생략한다. (강조하고 싶을 경우, 남겨 두는 것도 가능하다.)
  ② 주절의 주어와 부사절의 주어가 같으면, 부사절의 주어를 생략하고, 다르면 남긴다.
  ③ 부사절의 동사를 현재분사(동사원형-ing) 형태로 바꾼다.
  <u>Because I felt</u> tired, I took a nap. 나는 피곤했기 때문에 낮잠을 잤다.

  → <u>Feeling</u> tired, I took a nap.

  cf. 분사구문에서 being 뒤에 분사가 오면 being을 생략할 수 있다.

   (Being) tired from work, he went home early. 일이 피곤했기 때문에, 그는 집에 일찍왔다.

- **분사구문의 부정**: 분사 앞에 not이나 never를 써 준다.
  Not having enough money to take a taxi, they walked home.
  택시를 탈 충분한 돈이 없어서 그들은 집에 걸어갔다.

Point 06 분사구문은 시간, 원인, 조건, 동시상황 등을 나타내요!

- 시간   When I was young, I enjoyed playing soccer. 어릴 때 나는 축구를 즐겼었다.
     → Being young, I enjoyed playing soccer.

- 원인   Because I was sick, I didn't go shopping today. 아팠기 때문에, 나는 오늘 쇼핑하러 가지 않았다.
     → Being sick, I didn't go shopping today.

- 조건   If you turn left, you will see it on your right. 왼쪽으로 돌면 당신의 오른 편에서 볼 수 있습니다.
     → Turning left, you will see it on your right.

핵심만 콕! 문법 Check

A 〈보기〉와 같이 밑줄 친 현재분사인지 동명사인지 구분하시오.

> **보기**
> ① The <u>dancing</u> girl is my younger sister. (현재분사)
> ② My younger sister likes <u>dancing</u>. She is good at <u>dancing</u> hip-hop. (동명사)

1 <u>Barking</u> dogs seldom bite.   (현재분사, 동명사)

2 <u>Learning</u> a new language is fun.   (현재분사, 동명사)

3 He likes <u>reading</u> comic books.   (현재분사, 동명사)

B 두 문장의 뜻이 같도록 분사구문을 이용하여 바꿔 쓰시오.

1 After she finished her work, Jenny went to the gym to exercise.

→ _____, Jenny went to the gym to exercise.

2 Because he studied hard, he could pass the test.

→ _____, he could pass the test.

3 While I clean the room, I listen to music.

→ _____, I listen to music.

C 밑줄 친 부분을 괄호 안의 접속사를 사용하여 부사절로 바꿔 쓰시오.

1 <u>Seeing</u> us, he smiled brightly. (when)

→ _____, he smiled brightly.

2 <u>Being</u> late, he couldn't see the show. (because)

→ _____, he couldn't see the show.

3. <u>Leaving</u> right now, you won't be late. (if)

→ _____, you won't be late.

D 괄호 안의 말을 활용하여 분사구문이 들어간 문장을 완성하시오.

1 우리 차례를 기다리면서 우리는 TV를 보았다. (wait, our turn, for)

→ _____, we watched TV.

2 졸렸기 때문에 그녀는 수업에 집중할 수 없었다. (feel, sleepy)

→ _____, she couldn't concentrate on the class.

내신 만점! 실전 기출

01 빈칸에 알맞은 말을 고르시오.

The bag _____ by Susan is a bestselling item.

① design
② designing
③ designed
④ has designed
⑤ is designing

02 빈칸에 알맞은 말이 순서대로 바르게 나열된 것은?

We were very (A) _____ when we heard the news.
= The news was very (B) _____ to us.

① shock, shocking
② shocking, shocked
③ shocked, shocking
④ shocking, shocking
⑤ shocked, shocked

03 서술형

우리말과 일치하도록 괄호 안의 말을 바르게 배열하여 문장을 완성하시오.

문에 서 있는 여자가 내 여동생이야.
(standing, the woman, the door, at)

→ _____
_____ is my sister.

04 다음 밑줄 친 (A), (B)를 바르게 바꾸어 쓴 것으로 짝지어진 것은?

• We haven't (A) <u>finish</u> the project yet.
• I am thinking of (B) <u>buy</u> a new bag.

① finishing, buying
② finished, buying
③ finishing, bought
④ finished, bought
⑤ finish, buying

05 어법상 옳지 <u>않은</u> 것은?

① The story was very exciting.
② They were satisfying with the result.
③ It was a boring movie.
④ She must be very tired.
⑤ The class was interesting to me.

06 다음을 분사구문이 들어간 문장으로 바르게 바꿔 쓴 것을 고르면?

Because she felt tired, she stayed at home the whole day.

① She feeling tired, she stayed at home the whole day.
② Felt tiring, she stayed at home the whole day.
③ Being feeling tired, she stayed at home the whole day.
④ Feeling tired, she stayed at home the whole day.
⑤ Because felt tired, she stayed at home the whole day.

07 서술형

다음 두 문장을 분사구문을 이용하여 한 문장으로 바꿔 쓰시오.

Look at the children outside.
They are flying a kite.

→ Look at the children outside _____
_____.

08 밑줄 친 부분을 부사절로 바르게 바꾼 것은?

Not knowing how to swim, I don't like to go swimming.

① If I don't know how to swim,
② Since I don't know how to swim,
③ After I don't know how to swim,
④ Although I don't know how to swim,
⑤ Because I know how to swim,

09 밑줄 친 부분이 어법상 어색한 것은?

① Crossing the street, I saw them passing by.
② Surprising to hear the news, they screamed.
③ Entering the room, I turned on the radio.
④ Tired and sleepy, I decided to take a nap.
⑤ Satisfied with the result, he praised me.

최다빈출

10 밑줄 친 부분의 쓰임이 〈보기〉와 다른 것은?

보기
Look at the baby sleeping peacefully.

① She is waiting for me outside.
② I like the girl dancing on the stage.
③ I am not good at swimming.
④ I like to see her smiling.
⑤ They were packing the luggage.

11 빈칸에 알맞지 않은 것은?

Not bringing money, she couldn't buy anything.
→ _____ she didn't bring money, she couldn't buy anything.

① Because
② Since
③ As
④ When
⑤ Though

12 밑줄 친 부분의 쓰임이 어법상 틀린 것은?

① We felt the ground shaking.
② I had my hair permed.
③ They kept us waited for a long time.
④ I found my car broken.
⑤ She saw someone taking her wallet.

13 우리말과 뜻이 같도록 다음을 부정문으로 만들 때 'not'이 들어갈 위치로 알맞은 곳은?

수영하는 법을 몰라서 나는 수영장에 들어가지 않았다.

→ ① Knowing ② how ③ to swim ④, ⑤ I didn't get into the pool.

14 우리말을 영어로 바르게 옮긴 것은?

조용한 곳에 살고 싶어서 그는 시골로 이사했다.

① Because want to live in a quiet place, he moved to the countryside.
② Being wanted to live in a quiet place, he moved to the countryside.
③ Wanted to live in a quiet place, he moved to the countryside.
④ Wanting to live in a quiet place, he moved to the countryside.
⑤ Because wanted to live in a quiet place, he moved to the countryside.

15 서술형

빈칸에 공통으로 알맞은 말을 한 단어로 쓰시오.

> • _____ late for class again, I got scolded by my teacher.
> • _____ sleepy all of a sudden, she wanted to go home.

→ _____

16 서술형

주어진 문장과 같은 뜻이 되도록 괄호 안의 접속사를 이용하여 문장을 완성하시오.

> Being fixed, the cellphone worked without any problems. (after)

→ _____

17 밑줄 친 부분을 부사절로 바르게 바꾼 것은?

> Working hard, she couldn't meet the deadline.

① If she worked hard,
② Since she worked hard,
③ Because she worked hard,
④ Although she worked hard,
⑤ As she worked hard,

18 밑줄 친 부분이 어법상 어색한 것은?

① Having not money, I couldn't buy the clothes.
② Standing on the hill, I saw him leaving.
③ Being sleepy, I couldn't finish the homework.
④ Holding hands, they took a walk.
⑤ Doing his homework, he listened to music.

19 밑줄 친 부분의 쓰임이 다른 하나는?

① Working until late, she felt tired.
② Seeing a barking dog, he got scared.
③ Getting more pocket money, I became happy.
④ Memorizing all the Chinese letters makes me tired.
⑤ Not having enough time, they hurried up.

20 다음 밑줄 친 부분과 바꾸어 쓸 수 있는 것을 모두 고르면?

> Mom talked on the phone while she prepared dinner.

① she prepared
② while prepared
③ while preparing
④ while she preparing
⑤ preparing

21 어법상 옳지 않은 것은?

① Being late, he couldn't take the test.
② Going home late, he was scolded by his mom.
③ Disappointing, she cried a little.
④ Waiting for him, we had a chat on the bench.
⑤ Not good at cooking, I prefer to eat out.

신유형

22 밑줄 친 (A), (B)와 바꿔 쓸 수 있는 말이 순서대로 나열된 것은?

> • (A) Being angry, I yelled at my brother.
> • (B) Being angry, I didn't yell or shout.

① Because I was angry, Because I was angry
② Because I was angry, If I am angry
③ Although I was angry, Although I was angry
④ Although I was angry, Because I was angry
⑤ Because I was angry, Although I was angry

23 서술형

어법상 **틀린** 곳을 한군데 찾아 아래 조건에 맞도록 문장 전체를 고쳐 쓰시오.

┌─── 조건 ───────────────────────┐
1. 분사구문을 포함한 완전한 문장으로 쓸 것.
   (주절과 부사절의 주어는 같음)
2. 접속사를 생략할 것
3. 'Being'이 나오면 생략할 것
└────────────────────────────────┘

If using properly, the machine will help you a lot.

→ _____

_____

24 다음 대화의 밑줄 친 ⓐ~ⓔ중 어법상 **틀린** 것으로만 짝지어진 것은?

A: What are you reading?
B: Charlie and the Chocolate Factory.
   ⓐ It's very interesting.
A: Oh, ⓑ is it writing by Roald Dahl?
B: Yes, it is. I really like his novels.
   ⓒ His book is never bored.
A: You can say that again. Do you know that the novel was made into a movie?
B: Yes, but I haven't seen it yet.
A: ⓓ If you are interested, why don't we watch it after you're done with the novel?
B: ⓔ Sounds amazing.

① ⓐ, ⓑ
② ⓑ, ⓒ
③ ⓓ, ⓔ
④ ⓑ, ⓓ, ⓔ
⑤ ⓐ, ⓓ, ⓔ

25 서술형 심화

〈보기〉에서 알맞은 문장을 하나씩 골라 분사구문으로 형태를 바꿔 각 문장을 완성하시오. (단, 접속사는 생략)

┌─── 보기 ───────────────────────┐
ⓐ Although he cooks well,
ⓑ If you read English books an hour a day,
ⓒ Because she promised to go home together,
└────────────────────────────────┘

(1) _____,
you will be good at English soon.

(2) _____,
she was waiting for him.

(3) _____,
he likes eating out.

CHAPTER
05

시제

시제

어떤 일이 언제 어떤 식으로 일어나는지 시간 관계를 나타내는 것을 시제라 한다. 영어 문장에서 시제는 동사의 형태를 변화시켜 나타낸다.

• 시제

현재	She gets up early in the morning. 그녀는 아침에 일찍 일어난다.
과거	She got up late yesterday morning. 그녀는 어제 아침에 늦게 일어났다.
미래	She will get up early tomorrow. 그녀는 내일 일찍 일어날 것이다.
현재진행	She is reading a book now. 그녀는 지금 책을 읽고 있다.
과거진행	She was reading a book then. 그녀는 그 때 책을 읽고 있었다.
현재완료	She has read the book *Harry Potter*. 그녀는 "해리 포터"를 읽은 적이 있다.

한눈에 쏙! 문법 Chart

현재	(1) 현재의 사실이나 상태, 습관, 반복되는 일, 진리, 일반적 사실이나 진리, 속담 및 격언등을 나타낼 때	
	(2) 확정된 가까운 미래를 나타낼 때	
과거	과거의 행동이나 상태, 과거의 습관이나 관습, 과거의 역사적 사건 등을 나타낼 때	
	* 과거를 나타내는 부사(yesterday, last~, ago, in 과거 년도)가 있으면 반드시 과거시제로 쓴다.	
미래	미래에 대한 예측이나 의지, 요청:「will + 동사원형」	
	가까운 미래에 대한 계획을 나타낼 때:「be going to + 동사원형」=「will + 동사원형」	
진행	현재진행	(1) 현재 진행중인 일을 나타낼 때:「be동사의 현재형 + ~ing」
		(2) 확정된 가까운 미래의 일을 나타낼 때
	과거진행	과거 어느 시점에 진행 중이었던 일을 나타낼 때:「be동사의 과거형 + ~ing」
진행형으로 쓸 수 없는 동사들	(1) 감정/지각: hate, want, look, hear, smell, sound	
	(2) 사고/이해: think, believe, remember, know, understand	
	(3) 소유/소속: have, possess, belong to, own	
	(4) 상태: be, exist	
현재완료	과거에 일어난 일이나 상황이 현재와 관련되어 있을 때:「have(has) + p.p.」	
	의미: 경험, 완료, 계속, 결과	

핵심만 쏙! 문법 Point

Point 01 단순시제는 어느 한 때에 일어나는 일을 나타내요!

- 현재 시제는 현재의 사실이나 상태, 습관, 반복되는 일, 진리, 일반적 사실이나 진리, 속담 및 격언 등을 나타낼 때 쓴다.
  Mina does well in science. 미나는 과학을 잘 한다. (현재의 사실)
  The Earth goes round the sun. 지구는 태양 주위를 돈다. (일반적 사실이나 진리)
  A rolling stone gathers no moss. 구르는 돌에는 이끼가 끼지 않는다. (속담)

- 과거 시제는 과거의 행동이나 상태, 과거의 습관이나 관습, 과거의 역사적 사건 등을 나타낼 때 쓰이며, 과거를 나타내는 부사(yesterday, last~, ago, in 과거 년도)와 함께 쓰인다.
  Alice went home an hour ago. Alice는 한 시간 전에 집에 갔다.
  Neil Armstrong set foot on the moon in 1969. 닐 암스트롱은 1969년 달에 첫발을 내디뎠다.

- 미래에 대한 예측이나 의지, 요청 등을 나타낼 때 「will + 동사원형」으로 쓴다.
  부정형은 「will not (= won't) + 동사원형」, 의문문은 「will + 주어 + 동사원형~?」으로 쓴다.
  I will speak in English every day to improve my English.
  나는 영어를 향상시키기 위해 매일 영어로 말 할거야.
  We won't be late for school again. 우리는 다시 학교에 늦지 않을 거에요.
  What will you do this weekend? 너는 이번 주말에 무엇을 할거니?

Point 02 진행시제는 어느 순간에 진행중인 일을 나타내요!

- 현재 진행중인 일을 나타낼 때는 「be동사의 현재형 + ~ing」, 과거 어느 시점에 진행 중이었던 일을 나타낼 때는 「be동사의 과거형 + ~ing」구문을 쓴다.
  My father is reading a newspaper now. 아버지께서는 지금 신문을 읽고 계신다.
  Our teacher was calling our names one by one. 우리 선생님께서 우리들의 이름을 하나씩 부르고 계셨다.

- 확정된 가까운 미래의 일은 현재진행형으로 나타낼 수 있다.
  Are you coming to the party tonight? 오늘밤 파티에 오시나요?

- 두 동작이 동시에 진행될 때는 비교적 긴 동작을 진행형으로, 짧은 동작을 단순시제로 쓴다.
  What were you doing when I called you? 내가 전화했을 때 너 뭘 하고 있었니?

- 다음과 같은 뜻을 가진 동사는 대체로 진행형을 쓰지 않는다.

감정/지각	사고/이해	소유/소속	상태
hate 싫어하다 want 원하다 look ~하게 보이다 hear 들리다 smell ~한 냄새가 나다 sound ~하게 들리다	think 생각하다 believe 믿다 remember 기억하다 know 알다 understand 이해하다	have 가지다 possess 소유하다 belong to ~에 속하다 own 소유하다	be ~이다 exist 존재하다

- Don't you smell something burning? 너 혹시 타는 냄새 나지 않니?

- I think students need class rules. 나는 학생들에게 학급 규칙이 필요하다고 생각한다.
  주의! I am thinking about a solution now. (o) 나는 지금 해결책을 생각하고 있는 중이다. (임시 진행중인 동작)

핵심만 콕! 문법 Check

A 괄호 안에서 알맞은 말을 고르시오.

1 I (hear, heard) that the movie was very interesting.
2 The sun (rises, rose) in the east.
3 Sarah (wins, won) the dance contest last Friday.
4 Mina (rides, rode) a bike to school every day.
5 Walls (have, had) ears.

B 괄호 안의 단어를 활용하여 빈칸에 알맞은 형태로 바꿔 쓰시오.

1 My computer _____ very slowly. I want to buy a new one. (run)
2 My teacher said that water _____ at 0°C. (freeze)
3 The clothes _____ on sale now. (be)
4 The girl _____ her cat several days ago. (lose)
5 Last night, I _____ my parents about the plan. (tell)
6 I _____ _____ _____ _____ my homework by 6. (finish, going)

C 우리말과 뜻이 같도록 할 때 어법상 틀린 부분을 찾아 바르게 고쳐 쓰시오.

1 저는 지금 저희 아빠를 위한 셔츠를 찾고 있습니다.
  I am look for a shirt for my dad.   _____ → _____

2 걸어다니는 사전이란 모든 것을 아는 사람을 뜻한다.
  "Walking dictionary" meant a person who knows about everything.
                                                        _____ → _____

3 수진이는 수업이 때때로 지루하다고 생각한다.
  Sujin is thinking classes are sometimes boring.   _____ → _____

4 미국에 있는 내 사촌이 다음 달에 한국에 온다.
  My cousin in America is comes to Korea next month.   _____ → _____

5 그는 답을 찾기 위해 열심히 생각하고 있다.
  He thinks very hard to answer the question.   _____ → _____

D 괄호 안의 말을 활용하여 문장을 완성하시오. (필요하면 형태를 바꾸시오.)

1 너는 그 영화를 벌써 보았니? (see)
→ _____ the movie yet?

2 너는 지금 재미있는 시간을 보내고 있니? (have)
→ _____ fun now?

3 너는 한국에 대해서 어떻게 생각하니? (think)
→ What _____ of Korea?

핵심만 쏙! 문법 Point

Point 03 현재완료는 과거의 일이 현재까지 영향을 줄 때 써요!

- **현재완료란:** 과거에 일어난 일이나 상황이 현재와 관련되어 있음을 말할 때 사용한다. 현재완료의 형태는 「**have(has) + 동사의 과거분사(p.p.)**」이고, '**경험, 완료, 계속, 결과**'를 의미한다.
  Mr. Wilson has had many different jobs. Mr. Wilson은 여러 가지 직업을 가져왔다.

Point 04 현재완료는 완료, 경험, 계속, 결과를 의미해요!

- **완료:** '막~했다'의 의미로, 과거에 시작된 어떤 동작이 막 완료되었음을 나타낸다. **already, just, yet, now**등이 함께 온다. (just now는 과거 시제에 쓴다.)
  Jane has just finished her homework. Jane은 막 숙제를 끝냈다.

- **경험:** '~한 적이 있다'의 의미로, 현재까지의 경험을 나타낸다. 주로 **ever, never, before** 횟수를 나타내는 부사들과 등과 함께 쓰인다.
  Joanna has ridden a bike many times. Joanna는 자전거를 많이 타 봤다.

- **계속:** '지금까지 계속 ~해 왔다'의 의미로, 과거 어느 시점부터 현재까지 동작이나 상태가 계속되고 있음을 나타낸다. 주로 '**for + 기간**', '**since + 과거시점**' 등과 함께 쓰인다.
  We have studied English for three years. 우리는 3년동안 영어공부를 해 왔다.

- **결과:** '~해서 그 결과 ...되었다'의 의미로, 과거 사건이 현재에 영향을 미치고 있음을 나타낸다.
  Jake has lost his bike. Jake는 그의 자전거를 잃어 버렸다. (지금 자전거가 없음을 암시)
  (= Jake lost his bike, so he doesn't have it now.)

Point 05 현재완료의 have는 조동사와 같은 위치에 와요!

- 현재완료 부정문은 「**have not(never) + p.p.**」의 형태로 쓴다.
  We haven't met each other for a while. 우리는 한 동안 서로 만나지 못했다.

- 현재완료 의문문은 「**Have + 주어 + p.p. ~?**」, 혹은 「**의문사 + have + 주어 + p.p. ~?**」의 형태로 쓴다.
  Have you heard the news? 너 그 소식 들었니?
  How have you been? 너는 (그 동안) 어떻게 지냈니?

Point 06 현재완료는 현재와 과거가 관련 있고, 과거시제는 현재와 관련 없어요!

- 현재완료는 과거에 일어난 일이 현재까지 영향을 미치고 있음을 의미하는 반면에, 단순 과거 시제는 과거에 이미 끝난 일이며 현재와의 연관성을 내포하지 않는다.
  Mike lost his bike yesterday. Mike는 어제 그의 자전거를 잃어 버렸다. (현재 자전거가 있는지는 알 수 없음)
  Mike has lost his bike. Mike는 자전거를 잃어버렸다. (그 결과 현재 자전거가 없음)

- **현재완료와 함께 쓰지 않는 시간 부사:** yesterday, ago, last~, in 과거 년도 등과 같이 어떤 일이 분명한 과거 시점에 일어났음을 보여주는 시간 부사들은 현재완료에서 쓰이지 않는다. 일어난 사건의 시점을 물어보는 'When ~? (언제 ~?)'도 현재완료로 쓰지 않는다.
  When did you finish your homework? 넌 언제 숙제를 끝냈니?
  When have you finished your homework? (X)

  cf. 반면에 since, for 등은 현재완료와 함께 쓰인다.

핵심만 콕! 문법 Check

A 괄호 안에서 알맞은 말을 고르시오.

1 I (was, have been) a big fan of the Samsung Lions since I was a boy.

2 Susan (didn't finish, hasn't finished) her homework yet.

3 Jonnie (went, has been) to Europe several times.

4 English (was, has been) a global language for a long time.

B 다음을 현재완료 문장으로 바꿀 때, 빈칸에 알맞은 말을 쓰시오.

1 My father went to America, so he is not in Korea now.

→ My father _____ America.

2 Yumi started to learn dance two month ago. She is still learning it.

→ Yumi _____ dance _____ two months.

3 Mina went to Busan last week. That was her second time to go there.

→ Mina _____ Busan twice.

4 Hamin started to do his homework an hour ago. He just finished it.

→ Hamin _____ doing his homework.

C 밑줄 친 부분이 어법상 맞으면 O표, 틀리면 맞게 고쳐 쓰시오.

1 Dogs and cats <u>lived</u> with humans for a long time.   _____

2 She <u>has eaten</u> a hamburger yesterday.   _____

3 I <u>have gone</u> on a camping trip last week.   _____

4 When <u>have you been</u> in New York?   _____

5 Susan <u>never caught</u> a big fish so far.   _____

6 Yuri <u>came</u> to Korea three years ago.   _____

D 괄호 안의 말을 활용하여 문장을 완성하시오. (필요하면 형태를 바꾸시오.)

1 너는 쇼핑하러 가기 전에 구입할 물건 목록을 만들어 봤니? (made, you, have)

→ _____ a shopping list before you go shopping?

2 Jane은 일본에서 살아본 적이 있니? (lived, in, has, Japan, Jane)

→ _____ ?

3 Bill은 남대문 시장에 가 본 적이 없다. (been, to, before, has, Namdaemun Market, never)

→ Bill _____ .

4 너는 오늘 아침 이후로 무엇을 했니? (since, what, done, this, have, you, morning)

→ _____ ?

5 Jack은 숙제를 아직 끝내지 못했다. (not, homework, has, his, yet, finished)

→ Jack _____ .

내신 만점! 실전 기출

01 서술형

우리말과 같은 뜻이 되도록 빈칸에 알맞은 말을 쓰시오.

나는 이제부터 수업시간에 휴대폰을 사용하지 않을 것이다.

→ From now on, I _____ _____
_____ my cell phone in class.

02 빈칸에 알맞은 것을 고르시오.

Have you _____ Italian food?

① eat   ② ate   ③ eaten
④ eating   ⑤ to eat

03

A: Is this backpack Jane's?
B: Yes. She _____ it yesterday.

① buys   ② buys   ③ buying
④ bought   ⑤ has bought

04

When you called me, I _____ a book.

① read   ② was reading   ③ readed
④ to read   ⑤ have read

[5~6] 빈칸에 알맞은 말이 순서대로 바르게 짝지어진 것을 고르시오.

05

A: Have you studied English _____ a long time?
B: Yes. I have studied it _____ I was 7 years old.

① for, for   ② for, since
③ since, for   ④ since, when
⑤ when, since

06

A: Has Sujin been to America _____ ?
B: Yes. She went there three years _____ .

① ago, in 2013   ② before, in 2013
③ in 2013, ago   ④ before, ago
⑤ ago, before

07 서술형

두 문장의 의미가 같도록 주어진 단어를 사용하여 문장을 완성하시오.

Julie moved to New York five years ago, and she still lives there.

= Julie _____ _____ in New
York _____ five years. (live)

08 서술형

다음 우리말을 주어진 단어를 활용하여 영어로 쓰시오.
(필요하면 형태를 바꾸시오.)

Terry는 그의 방 청소를 막 끝냈다.
(clean, finish, just, have)

→ Terry _____
_____. (6단어)

09 빈칸에 알맞은 질문을 모두 고르면?

A: _____ ?
B: Last week.

① When did you finish it?
② Do you go there often?
③ How long have you studied English?
④ Since when has she started yoga?
⑤ When will John come back home?

10 빈칸에 알맞지 <u>않은</u> 것은?

A: What's your plan for the next year?
B: _____.

① I visited many countries.
② I want to go hiking with friends.
③ I will start learning taekwondo.
④ I hope to learn to play the violin.
⑤ I am going to exercise every day to get healthy.

[11~13] 〈보기〉의 밑줄 친 부분과 용법이 같은 것을 고르시오.

11

보기
<u>Have</u> you ever <u>done</u> any volunteer work before?

① Jack <u>has gone</u> to America.
② I <u>have lost</u> my notebook.
③ Tom <u>has written</u> his report.
④ Amy <u>has</u> never <u>been</u> to Europe.
⑤ Linda <u>has studied</u> Chinese for two years.

12

보기
They <u>have</u> just <u>arrived</u> at London.

① How <u>have</u> you <u>been</u> these days?
② She <u>has been</u> busy these days.
③ We <u>haven't seen</u> each other for a while.
④ Jina <u>has</u> already <u>finished</u> reading *The Last Leaf*.
⑤ The old man <u>has had</u> many different jobs.

13

보기
Cathy <u>has gone</u> shopping with her mom.

① I <u>have lost</u> my key.
② He <u>has</u> just <u>eaten</u> his breakfast.
③ My mom <u>has met</u> my friend Molly.
④ I <u>have known</u> him since I was a boy.
⑤ He <u>has written</u> books for children for years.

14 대화의 흐름이 자연스럽지 <u>않은</u> 것은?

① A: Have you seen this picture?
   B: No, I haven't.
② A: Has Sally gone home?
   B: Yes. She went home thirty minutes ago.
③ A: What did you do last night?
   B: I stayed home and watched TV.
④ A: What are you doing?
   B: I am just surfing the Internet.
⑤ A: What are you going to do this weekend?
   B: I visited my grandparents.

15 짝지어진 두 문장의 뜻이 같지 <u>않은</u> 것은?

① She went to Paris, so she is not here now.
   = She has been to Paris.
② Tom worked on his homework, and he is done with it now.
   = Tom has finished his homework.
③ Mary lost her purse, so she doesn't have it now.
   = Mary has lost her purse.
④ Sumin started volunteer work one year ago, and she is still doing it.
   = Sumin has done volunteer work for a year.
⑤ Mr. Brown started teaching in our school in March. He is still teaching us.
   = Mr. Brown has taught us since March.

16 서술형

주어진 낱말을 재배열하여 문장을 완성하시오.

Seoul, they, not, in, arrived, have, yet

→ _____

[17~18] 어법상 올바른 문장을 고르시오.

17

① I have went to the zoo twice.
② Susan has sick for a week.
③ He have lent me some money.
④ She has been not happy all day.
⑤ Emily has found the key to her house.

18

① When have you seen him?
② He has met her last Sunday.
③ The Korean War broke out in 1950.
④ Have you finished your report yesterday?
⑤ We have moved into this city three years ago.

19 어법상 어색한 것은?

① She ate Korean food last night.
② When have you finished your essay?
③ Janet has taught children since March.
④ Sarah and Sally have known each other for ten years.
⑤ Have you read the book *The Old Man and the Sea*?

20 어법상 올바른 문장을 모두 고르면?

① Time flies like an arrow.
② Mira is having two sisters.
③ One plus one equaled two.
④ Columbus discovers America.
⑤ I will become 15 years old next year.

[21~22] 다음 대화를 읽고 물음에 답하시오.

Jisu: You know what?
Mira: What?
Jisu: (A) The band 'Big Bang' is going to has a tour next month, and they are coming to Busan, too.
Mira: Wow! (B) You were a big fan of theirs since you were a girl, right?
Jisu: Yeah! (C) I am feeling so excited! Will you go to their concert with me?
Mira: What? (D) Won't we be busy preparing for our exams?
Jisu: Take it easy! Well, you know, (E) where there was a will, there was a way.

신유형

21 위 대화를 잘못 이해한 학생은?

① 수진: Big Bang이 다음 달에 순회공연을 할 계획이구나.
② 나연: Big Bang이 지금 부산으로 순회공연을 오고 있구나.
③ 민수: 지수는 어릴 때부터 Big Bang의 엄청난 팬이었구나.
④ 찬호: 지수는 Big Bang의 부산 순회공연에 매우 신이 나 있구나.
⑤ 수호: 미라와 지수는 곧 시험을 볼 예정이야.

22 위 대화의 밑줄 친 (A)~(E) 중 어법상 올바른 것은?

① (A)　　② (B)　　③ (C)　　④ (D)　　⑤ (E)

신유형

23 빈칸 (A)~(C)에 알맞은 말을 순서대로 바르게 나열한 것은?

> Jane wanted to help poor people in Africa. After she graduated from the college, she decided to teach poor African children. They (A) _____ to school. When she (B) _____ to Africa and saw children there, she felt sorry for them. Ever since then, she (C) _____ a great teacher to them.

① have never been, has been, was
② have never been, went, has been
③ never went, has gone, was
④ never went, went, has been
⑤ have never been, has gone, was

24 서술형

다음 내용과 일치하도록 빈칸에 알맞은 말을 쓰시오.

> Alice is planning a party tomorrow. She has to do several things to prepare for it.
>
> <Things to Do>
> 1. send invitation cards to friends (완료)
> 2. clean the living room (완료)
> 3. buy any snacks (미완료)

→ Alice has sent invitation cards to friends and

_____

_____ (5단어), but she _____

_____ (4단어) yet.

고난도

25 서술형 심화

다음 대화를 읽고 빈칸에 알맞은 말을 넣어 요약문을 완성하시오.

> Mary: Look! Those shorts look nice! Why don't you buy them?
> Amy: They look too small for me. I gained weight this year.
> Mary: Really? I'm sorry to hear that.
> Amy: I think I should lose weight. I will walk for 30 minutes every day.
> Mary: Good idea.

→ Amy (1) _____ weight, so she (2) _____

_____ for 30 minutes every day to lose weight.

CHAPTER

06

관계사

관계사

명사를 앞에서 꾸며주는 형용사처럼, 절(주어 + 동사 ~)을 이끌어 명사를 뒤에서 꾸며주는 말이다.
관계사에는 관계대명사, 관계부사 등이 있다.

● **관계사의 종류와 쓰임**

관계대명사	This is a book. → This is an interesting book. (형용사) → This is the book [which I read yesterday]. (목적격 관계대명사 절)
관계부사	I remember the place. → I remember the beautiful place. (형용사) → I remember the place [where I first met you]. (관계부사 절)

한눈에 쏙! 문법 Chart

관계대명사 종류	선행사가 사람일 때 : who – whose – whom 선행사가 사물, 동물일 때 : which – whose(of which) – which 선행사가 모든종류일 때 : that – whose - that
관계대명사 that만 쓸 때	선행사가 사람+사물, 최상급, 서수, the same, the only, the very를 포함할 때, 그리고 선행사가 –thing일 때
관계대명사 that이 못 올 때	관계대명사 앞에 전치사나 콤마(,)가 있을 때
관계대명사절의 구조	(1) 선행사 + 주격관계대명사 + (주어 생략됨) + 동사 (2) 선행사 + 목적격관계대명사 + 주어 + 동사 + (목적어 생략됨) (3) 선행사 + 소유격관계대명사 + 주어 + 동사 (생략된 문장 요소 없음) 　　　　　소유 관계
관계대명사 what	관계대명사 앞에 선행사(명사)가 없고, '~것'으로 해석됨
관계대명사 생략	(1) 목적격 관계대명사는 생략 가능 (단, 앞에 전치사가 있으면 불가) (2) 주격관계대명사가 뒤에 [be동사 + 분사]가 따라오는 경우는 [주격관계대명사 + be동사]를 　　함께 생략 가능
관계부사의 종류	when(시간), where(장소), why(이유), how(방법)

핵심만 쏙! 문법 Point

Point 01 관계대명사는 선행사의 종류에 따라 달라져요!

■ **관계대명사**는 「접속사 + 대명사」의 역할을 한다. 즉, 두 개의 절을 연결하는 동시에 앞에 나온 명사/명사(구)를 대신하는 것이다. 관계대명사가 이끄는 절은 선행사(= 앞에 오는 명사)를 수식한다. 관계대명사를 사용하여 두 개의 문장을 하나로 만드는 방법은 다음과 같다.

① 두 문장의 공통된 것을 찾아 삭제한다.	This is a story about a man. He helped poor African people. (a man = He) 이것은 어떤 남자에 대한 이야기이다. 그는 불쌍한 아프리카 사람들을 도왔다.
② 삭제된 명사와 격이 같은 관계대명사를 '선행사 다음, 뒤 문장 앞'의 위치에 놓는다.	This is a story about a man who helped poor African people. (삭제된 대명사가 사람(He)이고 주격이므로 who를 쓴다.) 이것은 불쌍한 아프리카 사람들을 도왔던 한 남자에 대한 이야기이다.

■ 관계대명사는 선행사의 종류에 따라 구분하여 쓰는 who, which, that 등이 있다.

선행사	주격	소유격	목적격
사람	who	whose	who(m)
사물, 동물, 개념	which	whose/of which	which
모든 종류	that	whose	that

Matt was the boy who was absent today.
Have you seen the movie which was titled *Star Wars*?
Are you looking for a boy and a dog that were at the park?
*주의: 선행사가 '사람+동물'이면 관계대명사 that을 쓴다.

Point 02 관계대명사 that은 선행사가 무엇이든 올 수 있어요!

■ **관계대명사 that**은 선행사의 종류에 관계없이 주격과 목적격으로 사용할 수 있다. 그러나 소유격으로는 사용하지 않는다. 또한 앞에 전치사와 콤마(,)가 오지 못한다.
Have you found the dog for that you were looking? (X) 네가 찾고 있던 개는 찾았니?

선행사가 사람 + 동물일 때	There are **many children and dogs** [that are playing in the park].
선행사가 최상급일 때	Blue whales are **the largest** animals [that grow up to 33m].
선행사에 서수가 포함되어 있을 때	John was **the first runner** [that reached the finish line].
선행사에 **the same, the only, the very**가 포함되어 있을 때	Mark is **the only student** [that got the full mark]. This is **the very bag** [that I am looking for].
선행사가 -thing으로 끝날 때	The man had **everything** [that I wanted to have].

핵심만 콕! 문법 Check

A 괄호 안에서 알맞은 말을 고르시오.

1 I saw a girl (who, whose) was taking the stairs instead of the elevator.
2 This is the man (whose, whom) job is selling cars.
3 Hong Kong is a city (whose, which) is one of the places to visit.
4 I saw the boy and his cat (which, that) you are looking for.

B 다음 두 문장을 관계대명사를 이용하여 한 문장으로 쓰시오.

1 I met a girl. She was my elementary school classmate.
→ I met a girl _____ was my elementary school classmate.

2 Sam is my classmate. His role is the prince in the play.
→ Sam is my classmate _____ role is the prince in the play.

3 I have seen the movie. It was titled Avatar.
→ I have seen the movie _____ was titled Avatar.

4 Usain Bolt is the fastest runner. He has many world records.
→ Usain Bolt is the fastest runner _____ has many world records.

C 다음 〈보기〉의 밑줄 친 that과 성격이 같으면 O, 다르면 X표 하시오.

> ┌─ 보기 ┌─
> Linda looks at the stars <u>that</u> shine brightly in the sky.

1 Did you hear <u>that</u> Tom became the school president?   → _____
2 He wanted to become an astronaut <u>that</u> much.   → _____
3 I like the picture <u>that</u> shows girls practicing the ballet.   → _____
4 <u>That</u> girl kicking the ball is my younger sister.   → _____
5 The motor show held in COEX wasn't <u>that</u> crowded yesterday. → _____
6 The problem is <u>that</u> she didn't arrive at the airport on time.   → _____
7 The woman <u>that</u> you are looking for is my teacher.   → _____

D 우리말과 같은 뜻이 되도록 괄호 안의 말을 이용하여 문장을 완성하시오.

1 반짝이는 모든 것이 금은 아니다. (glitter)
→ All _____ is not gold.

2 그녀가 한국어를 가르칠 수 있는 유일한 선생님이다. (teach, Korean, can)
→ She is the only teacher _____.

3 표지가 검은 색인 책을 좀 건네 주세요. (whose, cover, black, is)
→ Please pass me the book _____.

핵심만 쏙! 문법 Point

Point 03 관계대명사는 뒤에 오는 절에 무엇이 생략되었는지에 달렸다!

■ 관계대명사절의 구조는 다음과 같다.

(1) 관계대명사 바로 뒤에 「동사 + (목적어)」가 오면 주격 관계대명사가 필요하다.
   I know the boy [who is playing with the dog]. 나는 개와 함께 놀고 있는 소년을 안다.

(2) 관계대명사 바로 뒤에 「주어 + 동사」가 오면 목적격 관계대명사가 필요하다.
   I know the boy [who(m) you really like]. 나는 네가 매우 좋아하는 소년을 안다.

(3) 관계대명사 바로 뒤에 「주어 + 동사」이고, 선행사와 주어가 소유 관계이면 소유격 관계대명사가
   필요하다.
   The boy [whose hair is red over there] is my brother. 저기에 머리가 빨간 소년이 나의 동생이다.
   소유 관계

Point 04 관계대명사 what 앞에는 선행사가 없어요!

■ **관계대명사 what**은 선행사를 포함하는 관계대명사라서 앞에 명사(선행사)가 없다. 관계대명사 what은
  'the thing(s) that/which'로 바꿔 쓸 수 있다.
  This is not [what I ordered]. 이것은 제가 주문한 것이 아닙니다.
  = This is not the thing that(which) I ordered.
  cf. 주어로 쓰인 관계대명사 what절은 단수로 취급한다.

■ **관계대명사 what *vs.* 의문사 what**: '~것'으로 해석되면 관계대명사 what, '무엇'으로 해석되며 문장 안
  에서 가리키는 대상이 무엇인지 설명되지 않아 모를 때 묻는 것이 의문사 what이다.
  He showed me [what he had in his pocket]. (관계대명사)
  그는 나에게 주머니에 가지고 있던 것을 보여주었다.
  He asked [what I wanted to be]. 그는 나에게 무엇이 되고 싶은 지를 물었다. (의문사)

Point 05 목적격 관계대명사와 '주격관계대명사 + be동사'는 생략할 수 있어요!

■ 목적격 관계대명사 who(m), which, that은 생략할 수 있다. 단, 앞에 전치사가 있는 목적격 관계대명사의
  경우는 생략할 수 없다.
  She is eating spaghetti (which) her mom made. (which 생략 가능)
  I met the boy (whom(=who)) you told me about. (whom/who 생략 가능)
  = I met the boy about whom you told me. (whom 생략 불가)
  cf. 전치사가 앞에 온 목적격 관계대명사 whom의 경우는 who로 바꾸어 쓸 수 없다.
     I met the boy about who you told me. (X)

■ 주격관계대명사가 뒤에 [be동사 + 분사]가 따라오는 경우는 [주격관계대명사 + be동사]를 함께 생략할 수
  있다. 이 때, 관계대명사만 생략할 수는 없다.
  Do you know the girl ~~who is~~ dancing on the stage now? (O)
  Do you know the girl ~~who~~ is dancing on the stage now? (X)

핵심만 콕! 문법 Check

A 빈칸에 알맞은 관계대명사를 쓰시오. (단, 관계대명사 that은 쓰지 말 것.)

1 He bought a nice car _____ was from Germany.

2 Jessica is my friend _____ father is a singer.

3 John was the student _____ the teacher told to come early.

4 I want to have a dog _____ fur is very soft.

5 My mom made the cake _____ you are eating now.

6 It is a test for people _____ learn English.

7 The woman _____ I saw on the way home was Jessie.

B 두 문장의 뜻이 같도록 빈칸에 알맞은 말을 쓰시오.

1 She has lost the thing which I gave her.

    = She has lost _____ I gave her.

2 We won't forget the things that you did for us.

    = We won't forget _____ you did for us.

3 Tell me the thing that you want.

    = Tell me _____ _____ _____ .

C 우리말과 같은 뜻이 되도록 괄호 안의 말을 이용하여 문장을 완성하시오.

1 그는 내가 준 티셔츠를 입고 있다. (gave, I, him, to)

→ He is wearing the T-shirt _____ .

2 Janet은 John이 매우 좋아하는 소녀이다. (likes, John, really)

→ Janet is the girl _____ .

3 나는 영어로 쓰여진 책을 읽을 수 있다. (English, in, written)

→ I can read books _____ .

4 내가 이야기했던 그 남자는 매우 친절했다. (talked, I, to)

→ The man _____ was very friendly.

5 너는 그가 말한 것을 들었니? (said, he, what)

→ Did you hear _____ ?

6 너에게 나쁜 것들은 너무 많이 먹지 말아라. (that, the, are, things)

→ Don't eat too much of _____ not good for you.

핵심만 쏙! 문법 Point

Point 06 관계부사는 「전치사 + 관계대명사」와 같아요!

- **관계부사**는 [접속사 + 부사]의 기능을 하며, 관계부사절은 앞에 오는 명사(선행사)를 수식한다.
  관계부사는 [전치사 + 관계대명사]와 같다.

  (1) **관계부사 when:** 선행사가 시간을 나타내는 경우(the time, the day 등)에 쓴다.

  Do you remember the time? + We first met at the time.
  - → Do you remember the time <u>at which</u> we first met?
  - → Do you remember the time <u>when</u> we first met? 너는 우리가 처음 만난 때를 기억하니?

  (2) **관계부사 where:** 선행사가 장소를 나타내는 경우(the place, the city 등)에 쓴다.

  Tell me about the place. You first met your husband in the place.
  - → Tell me about the place <u>in which</u> you first met your husband.
  - → Tell me the place <u>where</u> you first met your husband. 남편을 처음 만난 곳에 대해 얘기해 주세요.

  (3) **관계부사 why:** 선행사가 이유를 나타내는 경우(the reason)에 쓴다.

  She didn't say the reason. She left early for the reason.
  - → She didn't say the reason <u>for which</u> she left early.
  - → She didn't say the reason <u>why</u> she left early. 그녀는 일찍 떠난 이유를 말하지 않았다.

  (4) **관계부사 how:** 선행사가 방법을 나타내는 경우(the way)에 쓴다.
  ※ 유의: the way와 how는 함께 쓰지 않는다.

  She didn't know the way. He could open the bottle in the way.
  - → She didn't know the way in which he could open the bottle.

    그녀는 그가 병을 연 방법을 몰랐다.
  - → She didn't know the way he could open the bottle. (O)

    = She didn't know how he could open the bottle. (O)

    * She didn't know the way how he could open the bottle. (X)

- 선행사와 관계부사는 둘 중 하나를 생략하기도 한다.

  This small village was the place where he was born. 이 작은 마을이 그가 태어난 곳이다.
  = This small village was the place he was born. (관계부사 생략됨)
  = This small village was where he was born. (선행사 생략됨)

핵심만 콕! 문법 Check

A 〈보기〉를 참고하여 두 문장의 뜻이 같도록 빈칸에 알맞은 말을 쓰시오.

> 보기
>
> He visited the city. He had lived in the city when he was young.
> = He visited the city <u>in which</u> he had lived when he was young.
> = He visited the city <u>where</u> he had lived when he was young.

1 I don't know the place. I lost my purse at the place.

→ I don't know the place _____ _____ I lost my purse.

→ I don't know the place _____ I lost my purse..

2 Would you tell me the time? You came to Korea at the time.

→ Would you tell me about the time _____ _____ you came to Korea?

→ Would you tell me about the time _____ you came to Korea?

3 Ask him the reason. He wants to borrow some money for the reason.

→ Ask him the reason _____ he wants to borrow some money.

4 She told me the way. I could plant potatoes in the way.

→ She told me _____ I could plant potatoes.

→ She told me _____ I could plant potatoes.

B 밑줄 친 부분이 어법상 맞으면 ○표, 틀리면 바르게 고치시오.

1 She didn't tell me the reason <u>why</u> she was late.　　　　　→ _____

2 Busan is the city <u>where</u> I lived in for a long time.　　　　→ _____

3 He could not figure out the way <u>how</u> the dog got out of the cage. → _____

4 He hasn't told us the day on <u>that</u> he will come back.　　　→ _____

5 The stream <u>in which</u> they played in was very shallow.　　→ _____

6 A zoo is where we can see many animals <u>there</u>.　　　　　→ _____

C 우리말과 같은 뜻이 되도록 괄호 안의 말을 이용하여 문장을 완성하시오.

1 금요일은 내가 봉사활동을 하는 날이다. (do, when, I)

→ Friday is the day _____ my volunteer work.

2 나의 아빠는 아침마다 그가 조깅하는 강변길로 가신다. (jogs, he, where)

→ My father goes to the riverside _____ every morning.

3 그것이 그가 학교에 늦은 이유이다. (for, was, the reason, he, which, for school, late)

→ That is _____.

4 그는 내가 복사할 수 있는 방법을 설명해 주었다. (I, make, how, a copy, could)

→ He explained _____.

5 Maria는 그녀가 학교 다니던 때를 기억한다. (was, she, when)

→ Maria remembers _____ at school.

01 빈칸에 알맞은 것을 고르시오.

> Mary knows the man _____ helped the poor old man.

① who   ② which   ③ whom
④ of which   ⑤ whose

02 서술형

다음 우리말과 뜻이 같도록 빈칸에 알맞은 말을 쓰시오.
(단, that은 쓰지 말 것)

> 코끼리는 긴 코를 가진 동물이다.

→ An elephant is an animal _____ has a long nose.

[3~5] 빈칸에 공통으로 알맞은 것을 고르시오.

03

> (1) She told me _____ she wanted to do.
> (2) _____ do you think of Korean foods?

① who   ② that   ③ what
④ which   ⑤ whom

04

> (1) He gave me something _____ I can use on a Halloween day.
> (2) Asako thinks _____ the Korean delivery system is very convenient.

① who   ② that   ③ what
④ which   ⑤ whom

05

> (1) I know the girl _____ is dancing on the stage now.
> (2) Did you hear _____ came here yesterday?

① who   ② that   ③ what
④ which   ⑤ whom

[6~7] 다음 문장을 관계대명사를 이용하여 한 개의 문장으로 바꾸어서 쓰시오.

06 서술형

> Korean meals often have many side dishes.
> + We don't finish them.

→ Korean meals often have many side dishes _____
_____. (4단어)

07 서술형

> The movie was interesting. + I watched it yesterday.

→ _____
_____.

[8~10] 〈보기〉의 밑줄 친 부분과 용법이 같은 것을 고르시오.

08

> 보기
>
> Children should listen to <u>what</u> their parents say.

① <u>What</u> a wonderful weather!
② <u>What</u> subject do you like most?
③ He didn't know <u>what</u> to choose.
④ <u>What</u> she wanted for lunch was spaghetti.
⑤ <u>What</u> do you think about Korean culture?

09

> 보기
>
> This is the book <u>that</u> I want to buy.

① How did you do <u>that</u>?
② Do you know <u>that</u> boy over there?
③ <u>That</u> is why he left without a word.
④ The house <u>that</u> has a red roof is my house.
⑤ The problem is <u>that</u> we don't have enough time.

10

> 보기
>
> The girl <u>who</u> is wearing blue jeans and a T-shirt is my sister.

① <u>Who</u> took my chair?
② I don't know <u>who</u> he was.
③ She didn't find <u>who</u> to talk to.
④ Look at the boy <u>who</u> has bright red hair.
⑤ My teacher asked me <u>who</u> I wanted to meet.

11 우리말과 뜻이 같도록 빈칸에 알맞은 말을 쓰시오.

침대 밑에 잠자고 있는 고양이가 있다.

→ (1) There is a cat _____

_____ sleeping under the bed.

공원에 축구를 하고 있는 소년들이 있다.

→ (2) There are boys _____

_____ playing soccer in the park.

최다빈출

[12~13] 어법상 올바른 문장을 고르시오.

12

① I received a china bowl which she made it last year.
② She has a cell phone that it has a nice camera.
③ The red dress that she is wearing is made of silk.
④ Mom is cooking dinner that it smells very delicious.
⑤ He is the boy who I met him yesterday at the park.

13

① Did you understand that I said?
② What I need now are some water.
③ This is the toy with which he played.
④ Tell me something what you know about it.
⑤ I will lend you the book who I am reading now.

14 서술형

우리말과 뜻이 같도록 빈칸에 알맞은 말을 쓰시오.

그가 원하는 것은 단지 짧은 휴식이었다.

→ _____

was just a short break. (3단어)

15 다음 밑줄 친 부분 중 생략할 수 있는 것을 모두 고르면? (2개)

① Please remember <u>what</u> I said to you.

② Music is the subject <u>which</u> I am interested in.

③ She made puppets <u>whose</u> bottoms are open.

④ A dacha is a house <u>that</u> Russians spend their weekends in.

⑤ John was the only student <u>that</u> finished the project in time.

16 빈칸에 that이 들어갈 수 없는 것은?

① Mira told me a funny story _____ I liked a lot.

② My friend really enjoyed the dishes _____ I made.

③ Antarctica is a place _____ weather is extremely cold.

④ The triathlon is a race for runners _____ are looking for a big challenge.

⑤ I volunteer for a group _____ helps elderly people at a nursing home.

17 다음 우리말을 영어로 옮길 때 빈칸에 알맞은 말은?

이 조각은 작가가 병뚜껑으로 만든 것이다.
→ This is a sculpture _____.

① the artist made that with bottle caps

② the artist made with that bottle caps

③ bottle caps that the artist made with

④ that the artist made with bottle caps

⑤ that bottle caps were made by the artist

[18~19] 다음 두 문장을 관계부사를 이용하여 한 문장으로 쓰시오.

18 서술형

This is the building.
My father works in this building.

→ This is the building _____
_____. (4단어)

19 서술형

That is the way.
She makes carrot cake in this way.

→ _____
_____. (7단어)

 최다빈출

[20~21] 어법상 어색한 것을 고르시오.

20

① He had buildings which were near Jongno.

② The bus which goes to Busan leaves at 2:40.

③ The trees which stands along the street are very tall.

④ She has two children who go to the same school with me.

⑤ Our teacher doesn't like a student who doesn't listen to him.

21

① Have you found the bag you lost?

② She has a cat which hair is dark grey.

③ The guide who I talked to was very nice.

④ He is a man whose job is to protect the forest.

⑤ Today was one of the most terrible days that I have had.

22 빈칸에 알맞은 말이 순서대로 바르게 나열된 것은?

> Yesterday, I saw a girl crying on the street on my way home. I asked her name and her house but I couldn't understand ⓐ _____ she said because she kept crying when she talked. I thought ⓑ _____ she must have been lost.

① what, what   ② what, that
③ which, what   ④ which, that
⑤ what, which

23 빈칸 ⓐ에 알맞은 단어와 그 쓰임이 같은 것을 <u>두 개</u> 고르면? (정답 2개)

> My teacher taught that there is not much water available for humans in the world. That's why there are many people ⓐ _____ don't have enough water in the world. So I decided to save water from now on.

① She played an oboe <u>that</u> made a soft sound.
② <u>Who</u> is the girl wearing a hairpin in her hair?
③ He did <u>that</u> because it would protect wild animals.
④ My brother doesn't like his hair color <u>that</u> much.
⑤ We are looking for a person <u>who</u> will teach children music.

24 〔서술형〕

우리말과 뜻이 같도록 주어진 단어를 바르게 배열하여 문장을 완성하시오.

> A: Have you been to Dokdo?
> B: No, I haven't.
> A: It is the farthest island from the east coast of Korea. Why don't we visit it next month?
> B: That sounds good. <u>there, go, we, the time, me, when, tell, can.</u>
> (우리가 거기에 갈 수 있는 때를 말해 줘.)
> A: OK. Let's check the calendar.

→ _____

_____

〔고난도〕

25 〔서술형 심화〕

A의 단어의 설명에 알맞은 내용을 B에서 골라 관계대명사를 사용하여 〈보기〉와 같이 문장을 완성하시오.

A	B
food	you can eat it in Mexico
animal	people in France speak it
language	we can see it in Alaska
house	it has lived with people for a long time

> 〔보기〕
> Tacos are <u>food which you can eat in Mexico</u>.

(1) A dog is _____

_____ .

(2) French is _____

_____ .

(3) An igloo is _____

_____ .

CHAPTER
07

수동태

수동태

주어와 동사가 어떤 관계인지 나타내는 형식을 '태 (Voice)'라고 하고, 능동태와 수동태, 두 가지가 있다. 주어가 동작을 스스로 하는 경우에는 능동태로 표현하고, 주어가 행동을 받거나 당하는 상황이면 수동태로 표현한다. 수동태의 동사는 「be동사 + 과거분사(p.p.)」형태로 나타낸다.

한눈에 쏙! 문법 Chart

능동태	주어(행위를 하는 것(사람)) + 동사 + 목적어 Hemingway wrote the great novel, *The Old Man and the Sea*.
수동태	주어(행위를 당하는 것(사람)) + be + p.p. (+ 목적어 생략(4형식 제외)) The great novel *The Old Man and the Sea* was written by Hemingway.

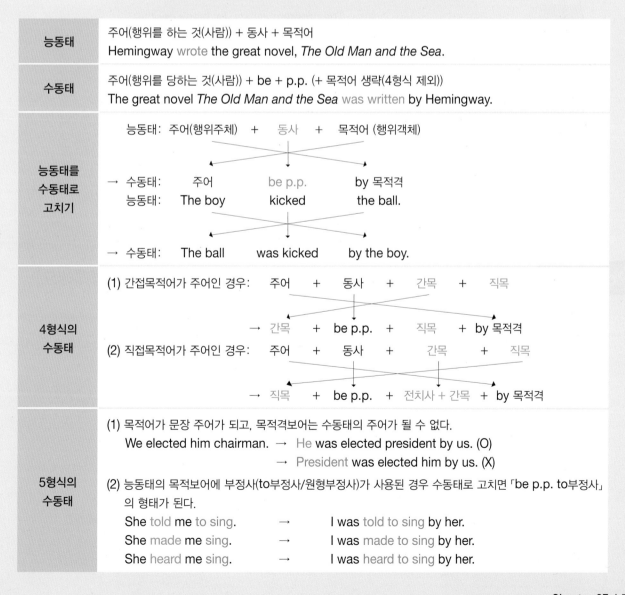

능동태를 수동태로 고치기	능동태: 주어(행위주체) + 동사 + 목적어 (행위객체) → 수동태: 주어 be p.p. by 목적격 능동태: The boy kicked the ball. → 수동태: The ball was kicked by the boy.
4형식의 수동태	(1) 간접목적어가 주어인 경우: 주어 + 동사 + 간목 + 직목 → 간목 + be p.p. + 직목 + by 목적격 (2) 직접목적어가 주어인 경우: 주어 + 동사 + 간목 + 직목 → 직목 + be p.p. + 전치사 + 간목 + by 목적격
5형식의 수동태	(1) 목적어가 문장 주어가 되고, 목적격보어는 수동태의 주어가 될 수 없다. We elected him chairman. → He was elected president by us. (O) → President was elected him by us. (X) (2) 능동태의 목적보어에 부정사(to부정사/원형부정사)가 사용된 경우 수동태로 고치면 「be p.p. to부정사」의 형태가 된다. She told me to sing. → I was told to sing by her. She made me sing. → I was made to sing by her. She heard me sing. → I was heard to sing by her.

핵심만 쏙! 문법 Point

Point 01 주어가 동사의 행동을 스스로 하면 능동태, 주어가 동사의 행동을 당하면 수동태에요!

- 수동태: 「주어 + be동사 + 과거분사(p.p.) + (by + 행위자)」
  The report was written by Mr. Lee. 그 보고서는 Mr. Lee에 의해 쓰여졌다.

- 능동태를 수동태로 바꾸는 방법은 다음과 같다.
  My grandfather built this house. 나의 할아버지께서는 이 집을 지으셨다.
  주어   동사   목적어

  This house was built by my grandfather. 이 집은 나의 할아버지에 의해 지어졌다.
  주어   동사   by+행위자
  ① 능동태의 목적어는 수동태의 주어로! ② 능동태의 동사는 be동사 + 과거분사(p.p.)의 형태로!
  ③ 능동태의 주어는 by + 목적격으로 문장 끝에!

Point 02 수동태의 시제는 be동사로 결정해요!

현재	am, are, is	+ 과거분사 (p.p.)	The program is seen by many people. 그 프로그램은 많은 사람들에 의해 보아진다.
과거	was, were		My bike was lost near the school. 내 자전거는 학교 근처에서 분실되었다.
미래	will be be going to be		The event will be delayed. 그 행사는 연기될 것이다. A new hall is going to be built. 새로운 전당이 지어지게 될 예정이다.

- 조동사가 있는 문장의 수동태는 「조동사 + be + 과거분사(p.p.)」의 형태로 쓴다.
  The road may be damaged by heavy rain. 그 도로는 폭우에 의해 손상을 입게 될 지도 모른다.
  The problem can be solved. 그 문제는 해결될 수 있다.

Point 03 수동태의 부정문은 「be동사 + not + 과거분사(p.p.)」의 형태에요!

현재	am/are/is + **not** + 과거분사(p.p.)	The supermarket is not closed. 그 슈퍼마켓은 문 닫혀있지 않다.
과거	was/were + **not** + 과거분사(p.p.)	The jewelry was not stolen. 그 보석은 도둑맞지 않았다.
미래	will **not** + be + 과거분사(p.p.)	The new product will not be launched soon. 새 상품이 곧 출시되지는 않을 것이다.
	be **not** going to + be + 과거분사(p.p.)	The bridge is not going to be built. 그 다리는 건설되지 않을 예정이다.

- 수동태의 의문문은 의문사가 있는지 없는지에 따라 형태가 다음과 같이 다르다.

의문사가 <u>없는</u> 경우	be동사 + 주어 + 과거분사(p.p.)~?	Are we invited to the party? 우리는 파티에 초대 되었나요?
의문사가 <u>있는</u> 경우	의문사 + be동사 + 주어 + 과거분사(p.p.)~?	When was this building built? 언제 이 건물이 지어졌나요?

핵심만 콕! 문법 Check

A 괄호 안에서 알맞은 말을 고르시오.

1 The presentation will (do, be done) by Ted.

2 The cat (feed, is fed) by my mom.

3 He (loved, is loved) by everyone.

4 My father (fixed, was fixed) my watch.

5 Romeo and Juliet (wrote, was written) by Shakespeare.

6 We (ordered, were ordered) pizza and chicken for dinner.

B 다음 문장을 수동태로 바꿀 때 빈칸에 알맞은 말을 쓰시오.

1 My father washed the car yesterday.

→ The car _____ by my father yesterday.

2 The earthquake destroyed many buildings in that area.

→ Many buildings in that area _____ by the earthquake.

3 Jack will make a speech tomorrow.

→ A speech _____ by Jack tomorrow.

C 다음 우리말과 뜻이 같도록 괄호 안의 말을 활용하여 문장을 완성하시오.

1 영어는 많은 나라에서 말하여진다. (speak)

→ English _____ in many countries.

2 전구는 Edison에 의해 발명되었다. (invent)

→ The lightbulb _____ by Edison.

3 이 노래는 작년에 많은 가수들에 의해 불려졌다. (sing)

→ The song _____ by many singers last year.

D 괄호 안에서 알맞은 말을 골라 문장을 다시 쓰시오.

1 These products (was, were) not made in Korea.

→ _____

2 (Did, Was) this computer fixed by him?

→ _____

3 (Do, Are) these rooms cleaned every day?

→ _____

핵심만 쏙! 문법 Point

Point 04 4형식 문장의 수동태는 두 가지의 형태가 가능해요!

능동태(4형식 문장)	John gave <u>me great advice</u>. John은 나에게 아주 좋은 조언을 해주었다. 간·목　　직·목
간접목적어가 주어인 수동태	I was given great advice by John. 나는 John에 의해 아주 좋은 조언을 받았다.
직접목적어가 주어인 수동태 (간목 앞에 to, for, of를 쓴다.)	Great advice was given to me by John. 아주 좋은 조언이 John에 의해 나에게 주어졌다.

Point 05 5형식 문장(주어 + 동사 + 목적어 + 목적격 보어)을 수동태로 바꿀 때 목적어를 주어로 쓰고 보어는 그대로 남겨요! 보어는 수동태의 주어로 쓸 수 없어요!

Most of us think Terry a very smart student. (능동태)
우리 대부분은 Terry를 매우 영리한 학생으로 생각한다.
Terry is thought a very smart student by most of us. (수동태)
Terry는 우리 대부분에 의해 매우 영리한 학생으로 여겨진다.

Point 06 지각동사가 쓰인 5형식 문장의 수동태에서 목적격 보어(동사원형)는 to부정사가 돼요!

We heard the woman scream. 우리는 그 여자가 소리지르는 것을 들었다.
→ The woman was heard to scream by us. 그 여자는 우리에 의해 소리지르는 것이 들려졌다.

Point 07 사역동사가 쓰인 5형식 문장의 수동태에서 동사는 다음과 같아요!

make	be made to	～하도록 되다
have	be asked to	～하기를 부탁받다
let	be allowed to	～하는 것을 허락받다

She made us finish the meal. 그녀는 우리가 식사를 끝마치도록 시켰다.
→ We were made to finish the meal by her. 우리는 그녀에 의해 식사를 끝마치게 되었다.

Point 08 구동사가 있는 능동태 문장을 수동태로 바꿀 경우 구동사를 한 단어처럼 써요! 이 때, 전치사를 빠뜨리지 않도록 유의해야 해요!

We took care of the dog. 우리가 그 개를 돌보았다.
→ The dog was taken care of by us. 그 개는 우리에 의해 돌보아졌다.
The kids will be brought up by their grandmother. 그 아이들은 그들의 할머니에 의해 길러질 것이다.

Point 09 by 대신 다른 전치사를 쓰는 경우는 다음과 같아요!

be surprised at	～에 놀라다	be pleased with	～에 기뻐하다
be known to	～에게 알려져 있다	be bored with	～에 싫증나다
be known as	～로서 알려져 있다 (자격)	be tired of	～에 싫증나다
be known for	～때문에 알려져 있다 (이유)	be scared of	～을 두려워하다
be made of/from	～으로 만들어지다	be prepared for	～에 대해 준비되다
be interested in	～에 관심 있다	be filled with	～으로 가득 차다
be satisfied with	～에 만족하다	be dressed in	～으로 차려 입다
be disappointed with	～에 실망하다	be covered with	～으로 덮여 있다

핵심만 콕! 문법 Check

A 다음 4형식, 5형식 수동태 문장의 밑줄 친 부분을 어법에 맞게 고쳐 문장 전체를 다시 쓰시오.

1 Some chocolates were <u>made me</u> by Yuna.

→ _____

2 A love letter was <u>sent for her</u> by someone.

→ _____

3 He was <u>elected to president</u> by them.

→ _____

B 우리말과 뜻이 같도록 괄호 안의 말을 바르게 배열하여 문장을 완성 하시오.

1 Peter는 엄마에게 약간의 용돈을 받았다. (given, was, his mom, by, allowances, some)

→ Peter _____.

2 약간의 용돈이 엄마에 의해 Peter에게 주어졌다. (were, by, his mom, given, to, Peter)

→ Some allowances _____.

3 재미있는 이야기가 그의 의해 우리에게 들려졌다. (was, to, us, told, by, him)

→ A funny story _____.

C 다음 능동태 문장을 수동태 문장으로 바꾸시오.

1 Mom looked after the puppy.

→ _____

2 They should not look down on him.

→ _____

3 Jenny takes care of her grandmother.

→ _____

D 〈보기〉에서 빈칸에 알맞은 한 단어를 찾아 빈 칸에 쓰시오.

보기				
with	at	in	of	to

1 She is interested _____ Chinese culture.

2 They were all surprised _____ the news.

3 I was satisfied _____ my score.

4 We were all scared _____ bees.

5 Mr. Lee's capability was well known _____ many people.

01 빈칸에 알맞은 것을 고르시오.

The errors in the report _____ by my teacher.

① correct
② corrected
③ was corrected
④ were corrected
⑤ be corrected

02 서술형

두 문장이 같은 뜻이 되도록 빈칸에 알맞은 말을 쓰시오.

Many people enjoy Korean movies these days.

→ Korean movies _____
_____ by many people these days.

03 다음 중 어법상 올바른 문장은?

① This poem did written by Kate.
② This machine was use to make ice.
③ Your gift will be liked by them.
④ This car isn't be made in Japan.
⑤ He will praise by his teacher.

04 빈칸에 알맞은 것은?

I think less money _____ on buying furniture.

① should spend
② should spent
③ should be spent
④ should is spent
⑤ should have spent

05 다음 문장을 수동태로 바르게 고친 것을 고르시오.

He invited us to his birthday party.

① We are invited to his birthday party by him.
② We invited to his birthday party by him.
③ We were invite to his birthday party by him.
④ We were invited to his birthday party by him.
⑤ We invited him to his birthday party.

06 서술형

우리말과 일치하도록 문장에서 틀린 부분을 고쳐 바르게 쓰시오.

그 숙제는 이번 주 금요일까지 완성 되어야 한다.
The homework must complete by this Friday.

→ _____

07 다음 우리말을 영어로 바르게 옮긴 것은?

월드컵은 4년마다 개최된다.

① The World Cup hold every 4 years.
② The World Cup held every 4 years.
③ The World Cup is hold every 4 years.
④ The World Cup is held every 4 years.
⑤ The World Cup will is held every 4 years.

최다빈출

08 어법상 틀린 문장은?

① The pizza will be delivered soon.
② The painting was given to me.
③ His new book will publish.
④ The promise between us was broken.
⑤ The door is locked.

09 서술형

괄호 안에 주어진 동사를 활용하여 우리말과 뜻이 같도록 빈칸에 알맞은 말을 쓰시오.

그들은 할머니에 의해 길러졌다. (bring up)

→ They _____
_____ their grandmother.

10 다음 의문문을 수동태로 바르게 고친 것은?

Does someone clean these rooms every day?

① Do these rooms cleaned every day?
② Are these rooms clean every day?
③ Are these rooms cleaned every day?
④ By whom are these rooms cleaned every day?
⑤ Is someone cleaned these rooms every day?

11 다음 중 수동태로 바꿀 수 <u>없는</u> 문장은?

① Somebody stole his wallet.
② They brought us some books.
③ His lecture made people interested.
④ They saw me talk to the teacher.
⑤ I woke up late this morning.

12 다음 문장을 능동태로 바르게 고친 것은?

I was made to tell the secret by her.

① I made her to tell the secret.
② I made her tell the secret.
③ She made me to tell the secret.
④ She made me tell the secret.
⑤ She told me the secret.

13 다음 문장을 수동태로 바르게 고친 것은?

Lisa told me some interesting stories about her childhood.

① Some interesting stories about her childhood was told me by Lisa.
② Some interesting stories about her childhood is told me by Lisa.
③ Some interesting stories about her childhood was told to me by Lisa.
④ Some interesting stories about her childhood were told to me by Lisa.
⑤ Some interesting stories about her childhood were told me by Lisa.

14 빈칸에 알맞은 말이 순서대로 바르게 나열한 것은?

• He seems satisfied ⓐ _____ my answer.
• It snowed a lot last night, so the road is covered ⓑ _____ the snow.

① to, by   ② for, by   ③ at, at
④ with, with   ⑤ by, with

15 밑줄 친 단어의 올바른 형태를 순서대로 바르게 나열한 것은?

• They were seen ⓐ <u>enter</u> the teacher's room.
• I was made ⓑ <u>apologize</u> to my sister.

① enter, apologize   ② to enter, to apologize
③ to enter, apologize   ④ enter, to apologize
⑤ entering, apologizing

16 서술형

우리말과 뜻이 같도록 괄호 안의 단어를 바르게 배열하여 문장을 완성하시오.

음식을 먹는 것이 도서관에서 허용되어서는 안 된다.
(should, be, not, allowed, eating, food)

→ _____
_____ in the library.

17 밑줄 친 부분을 주어로 하여 수동태로 만들 수 <u>없는</u> 문장은?

① We call him <u>a genius</u>.
② He showed <u>his ticket</u> to the man.
③ Our teacher told <u>us</u> not to be late.
④ She warned <u>them</u> not to make a noise.
⑤ They brought <u>a cute puppy</u> home.

18 빈칸에 알맞은 말이 나머지와 다른 하나는?

① We were pleased _____ the result.
② His face was filled _____ happiness.
③ They must be disappointed _____ my behavior.
④ He looks satisfied _____ his job.
⑤ We are tired _____ the same dish every day.

19 짝지어진 두 문장의 의미가 같지 <u>않은</u> 것은?

① My mother made me clean the room.
   → I was made to clean the room by my mother.
② The doctor advised us not to eat junk food.
   → We were advised not to eat junk food by the doctor.
③ They gave me some bread and hot tea.
   → I was given some bread and hot tea by them.
④ My father bought me these glasses.
   → These glasses were bought for me by my father.
⑤ They elected him president.
   → The president was elected by him.

20 빈칸 ⓐ~ⓒ에 알맞은 말을 골라 순서대로 바르게 나열한 것은?

> ⓐ They were all satisfied (with, by) the food he made.
> ⓑ He was made (to stop, stopping) by the police.
> ⓒ We were heard (to chat, chat) by teacher.

① with, to stop, chat
② with, stopping, chat
③ with, to stop, to chat
④ by, to stop, to chat
⑤ by, stopping, chat

21 서술형

괄호 안의 말을 활용하여 〈보기〉와 같이 수동태 문장을 만드시오.

┌─── 보기 ────────────────────
│ the glass / break / John (과거시제)
│ → The glass was broken by John.
└────────────────────────────

the bread / bake / I (과거시제)

→ _____

22 다음 글에서 어법상 틀린 것을 찾아 바르게 고친 사람은?

Hangeul ⓐ <u>was created</u> by King Sejong in 1443. At that time, most people ⓑ <u>couldn't read or write</u> because books ⓒ <u>were written</u> in Chinese characters, Hanja. Hanja was very difficult to read. King Sejong thought it was necessary to create our own characters. Scholars in Jiphyunjeon ⓓ <u>asked</u> to create scientific and easy-to-read characters by him. And they were able to ⓔ <u>create</u> Hangeul in the end.

① 민지: ⓐ was created를 created로 고쳐야 해.
② 소은: ⓑ couldn't read or write를 couldn't be read and written으로 고쳐야 해.
③ 미나: ⓒ were written을 wrote로 고쳐야 해.
④ 한나: ⓓ asked를 were asked로 고쳐야 해.
⑤ 유라: ⓔ create을 be created로 고쳐야 해.

23 서술형

우리말과 뜻이 같도록 괄호 안의 말을 활용하여 대화를 완성하시오.

> Tom: ⓐ 새로운 007 영화가 곧 개봉될 거야.
> (a new 007 movie, be, release, soon)
> Jack: I saw the preview and ⓑ 나는 깊은 감명을 받았어. (deeply, be, impress)
> Tom: Really? I am really looking forward to seeing it.

→ ⓐ _____

→ ⓑ _____

24 서술형

밑줄 친 부분을 어법에 맞게 고쳐 쓰시오.

> Have you ever heard about Busan? Busan ⓐ <u>locates</u> in Korea. It ⓑ <u>is known at</u> many people around the world because of the Busan International Film Festival. The film festival ⓒ <u>hold</u> in Busan in October every year. Come and see the festival in Busan!

→ ⓐ _____

→ ⓑ _____

→ ⓒ _____

25 서술형 심화

Complete the dialogue based on the picture. Use the given word.

(1)

Q: Were there many books on the bookshelf?

A: Yes. The bookshelf _____ _____ a lot of books. (fill)

(2)

Q: What was impressive about the mountains?

A: The scenery was beautiful. The mountains _____ _____ snow. (cover)

CHAPTER
08

가정법

가정법

실제 일어나지 않은 일에 대해 반대로 가정해서 자신의 의견이나 소망을 표현하는 방법이 가정법(假定法)이다. 즉, 거짓으로(假) 정하여(定) 표현하는 방법(法)을 뜻한다. 이렇게 사실과 다르게 표현하는 장치로써, 말하는 기준 시점보다 한 단계 이전의 시제를 쓴다.

• 가정법의 종류

현재 사실과 반대로 가정하는 '가정법 과거'와, 과거 사실과 반대로 가정하는 '가정법 과거완료'가 있다.

가정법 과거	If I were on the Arctic land now, I could see aurora. → 직설법: As I am not on the Arctic land now, I can't see aurora.
가정법 과거완료	If the goalkeeper hadn't missed the ball, our team could have won the game. → 직설법: As the goalkeeper missed the ball, our team couldn't win the game.

한눈에 쏙! 문법 Chart

가정법 과거	현재의 사실과 반대되는 상황이나 실현 가능성이 낮은 일을 가정할 때 「If + 주어 + 동사의 과거 ～, 주어 + 조동사의 과거형 + 동사원형 …」 '만일 ～라면, …할 텐데' * 단순조건문(If절에 현재시제가 쓰이는 경우)는 실현될 가능성이 있을 때 쓴다.
가정법 과거완료	과거의 사실과 반대되는 상황을 가정할 때 「If + 주어 + had p.p. ～, 주어 + 조동사의 과거형 + have p.p. …」 '만일 ～했다면, …했을 텐데'
I wish 가정법 과거	현재나 미래에서 실현될 수 없는 소망이나, 현재 사실에 대한 유감을 나타낼 때 「I wish + 주어 + 동사의 과거 …」 '～라면 좋을 텐데'
I wish 가정법 과거완료	과거에 이루지 못했던 일에 대한 후회나 아쉬움을 나타낼 때 「I wish + 주어 + had p.p. …」 '～했다면(이었다면) 좋았을 텐데'
as if 가정법 과거	실제로 말을 하고 있는 당시의 사실은 그렇지 않은데, 마치 그런 것처럼 보인다고 표현할 때 「as if + 주어 + 동사의 과거 …」 '마치 …인 것처럼'
as if 가정법 과거완료	과거에 실제로는 그렇지 않았는데 마치 그랬던 것처럼 보인다고 표현할 때 「as if + 주어 + had p.p.」 '～마치 …했던(이었던) 것처럼'

핵심만 쏙! 문법 Point

Point 01 가정법 과거는 현재의 사실과 반대되는 가정을 할 때 써요!

■ **가정법 과거**는 현재의 사실과 반대되는 상황이나 실현 가능성이 낮은 일을 가정할 때 쓴다.

> 「If + 주어 + <u>동사의 과거</u> ~, 주어 + <u>조동사의 과거형</u> + **동사원형** …」 '만일 ～라면, …할 텐데'
> would/could/should/might

※ 유의: 가정법인 if절의 동사가 be동사이면, 주어의 인칭과 수에 상관 없이 항상 **were**를 쓴다.
If I spoke English fluently, I could communicate freely with people from other countries.
내가 만일 영어를 유창하게 말할 수 있다면, 나는 외국인들과 자유롭게 의사 소통할 수 있을 텐데.
If I were a bird, I could fly high in the sky. 내가 만일 새라면, 하늘 높이 날 수 있을 텐데.

■ **가정법 → 직설법 전환** 방법은 과거시제를 현재시제로 고치고, 긍정문이면 부정문으로, 부정문이면 긍정문으로 바꾼다.
If I <u>had</u> enough money, I <u>wouldn't have</u> to borrow some money. (가정법)
    ①   ②   내가 충분한 돈이 있다면, 돈을 빌릴 필요가 없을 텐데.
→ As I <u>don't have</u> enough money, I <u>have to</u> borrow some money. (직설법)
내가 충분한 돈이 없어서, 돈을 좀 빌려야만 한다.
① 가정법 if절의 동사 과거형(had)을 현재형(have)으로 바꾸고, 가정법에 not이 없으므로 직설법에는 넣는다.
② 가정법 주절의 동사를 현재시제로 바꾸고, 가정법에 not이 있으므로 직설법에는 뺀다.

■ **단순 조건문 vs. 가정법 문장** '～라면'이라는 뜻의 접속사 if는 조건을 말할 때(단순 조건문), 가정할 때 (가정법) 둘 다 쓴다. 조건문과 가정법의 의미상 차이는 '실현 가능성'에 있다.

(1) **단순 조건문**: 조건이 충족되면, 실현될 가능성이 있음. 「If + 주어 + **동사의 현재형**, 주어 + **조동사의 현재형 + 동사원형**」으로 쓴다.
If he has enough money, he will buy the car. (충분한 돈을 가지고 있을 수도 있다고 생각함)
그가 충분한 돈이 있다면, 그 차를 살 것이다.

(2) **가정법**: 실현 불가능한 일을 가정. 「If + 주어 + **동사의 과거형**, 주어 + **조동사의 과거형 + 동사원형**」으로 쓴다.
If he had enough money, he would buy the car. (충분한 돈이 없음)
그가 (만약에) 충분한 돈이 있다면, 그 차를 살 텐데. (충분한 돈이 없어서 그 차를 살 수 없음)

Point 02 가정법 과거완료는 과거의 사실과 반대되는 사실을 가정할 때 써요!

■ 과거의 사실과 반대되는 상황을 가정할 때 쓴다.

> 「If + 주어 + <u>**had p.p.**</u> ~, 주어 + **조동사의 과거형** + <u>**have p.p.**</u> …」 '만일 ～했다면, …했을 텐데'
> would/could/should/might

If it <u>hadn't rained</u>, our field trip <u>wouldn't have been</u> canceled. 비가 오지 않았더라면, 체험학습은
        ①   ②   취소되지 않았을 텐데.
→ As it <u>rained</u>, our field trip <u>was</u> canceled. 비가 와서 체험학습이 취소되었다.
① if절의 과거완료시제(hadn't rained)를 과거시제(rained)로 바꾸고, 가정법에 not이 있으므로 직설법에서는 뺀다.
② 주절의 would have p.p.를 과거시제(was)로 바꾸고, 가정법에 not이 있으므로 직설법에서는 뺀다.

핵심만 콕! 문법 Check

A 괄호 안에서 알맞은 말을 고르시오.

1 If I (am, were) in Paris now, I could visit the Louvre Museum.

2 If Jane (is, were) at home, she will answer the phone.

3 If John (has, had) time, he would go out with me.

4 If he (had, had had) free time, he would have come to play basketball.

5 If Jack had come here, we could (practice, have practiced) badminton together.

6 If I (knew, had known) your email address, I would have sent it to you.

7 If she had read the book, she would (know, have known) the story.

8 If you hadn't watched TV, you could (finish, have finished) your homework.

B 두 문장의 의미가 같도록 문장을 완성하시오.

1 If I were free now, I could watch a movie.

→ As I _____ free now, I _____ watch a movie.

2 If he liked her, he would ask her to go out with him.

→ As he _____ her, he _____ her to go out with him.

3 If you had been there, you could have joined the game.

→ As you _____ there, you _____ the game.

4 If it hadn't rained, the game would have been held.

→ As it _____, the game _____.

5 If you hadn't watered the plants, they would have died.

→ As you _____ the plants, they _____.

C 괄호 안의 말을 활용하여 문장을 완성하시오.

1 If it _____ sunny tomorrow, we will play soccer. (be)

2 If you hadn't helped me, I _____ _____ _____ the job. (finish)

3 If he _____ _____ something to do, he wouldn't have come to the concert. (have)

4 If he had enough time, he _____ _____ it a lot better. (do)

5 If I had been tired, I _____ _____ _____ home. (stay)

6 If Bill _____ the living room, it would have been messy. (clean)

핵심만 쏙! 문법 Point

Point 03 「I wish + 가정법」은 현재나 과거의 사실을 반대로 소망함을 의미해요!

- 「I wish + 가정법 과거」는 현재나 미래에서 실현될 수 없는 소망이나, 현재 사실에 대한 유감을 나타낸다.

  「I wish + 주어 + 동사의 과거형 …」 '~라면 좋을 텐데'
  → 가정법의 동사가 be동사일 때는 인칭에 관계없이 항상 were를 쓴다.
  → 직설법: 「I am sorry(that) + 주어 + 동사의 현재형」

  ※ 직설법으로 고칠 때, 가정법 문장의 과거 시제를 현재 시제로 고치고,
    가정법 문장이 긍정문이면 부정문으로, 부정문이면 긍정문으로 바꾼다.
    I wish I had a little brother like Minho. 민호 같은 남동생이 있다면 좋을 텐데.

    → I am sorry (that) I don't have a little brother like Minho.
      민호 같은 남동생이 없다는 것이 유감이다.

- 「I wish + 가정법 과거완료」는 과거에 이루지 못했던 일에 대한 후회나 아쉬움을 나타낼 때 쓰인다.

  「I wish + 주어 + had p.p. …」 '~했다면(이었다면) 좋았을 텐데'
  → 직설법: 「I'm sorry (that) + 주어 + 동사의 과거형 …」

  I wish I had been a good sister. 내가 좋은 언니였더라면 좋았을 텐데.

  → I am sorry (that) I wasn't a good sister. 내가 좋은 언니가 아니었던 것이 후회스럽다.

Point 04 「as if + 가정법」은 현재 혹은 과거의 사실과 반대임을 의미할 때 써요!

- 「as if + 가정법 과거」는 실제로 말을 하고 있는 당시의 사실은 그렇지 않은데, 마치 그런 것처럼 보인다고 표현할 때 쓴다. 이 때 as if절의 내용은 주절의 시제와 같은 시점의 일이다.

  「as if + 주어 + 동사의 과거 …」 '마치 …인 것처럼'

  He acts as if he were a superman. 그는 마치 자신이 슈퍼맨인 것처럼 행동한다.

  → In fact, he is not a superman. 사실은, 그는 슈퍼맨이 아니다.

- 「as if + 가정법 과거완료」는 말하는 당시를 기준으로, 과거에 실제로는 그렇지 않았는데 마치 그랬던 것처럼 보인다고 표현할 때 쓰인다. 이 때 as if절의 내용은 주절보다 한 시제 앞선 시점의 일이다.

  「as if + 주어 + had p.p.」 '~마치 …했던(이었던) 것처럼'

  He talks as if he had been a school president. 그는 마치 자신이 학생 회장이었던 것처럼 말한다.

  → In fact, he was not a school president. 사실은, 그는 학생회장이 아니었다.

핵심만 콕! 문법 Check

A 괄호 안에서 알맞은 말을 고르시오.

1 I wish I (did, had done) better on the English exam yesterday.

2 I wish my mom (were, had been) at home now.

3 I wish you (were, had been) with me then.

4 I wish I (didn't fight, hadn't fought) with my friend last week.

B 두 문장의 의미가 같도록 문장을 완성하시오.

1 I am sorry I am the older child.

→ I wish _____ the older child.

2 I am sorry I don't know where he lives.

→ I wish _____ where he lives.

3 I wish I had joined the club.

→ I am sorry _____ the club.

4 I wish the snow hadn't melted into water.

→ I am sorry the snow _____ into water.

5 He looks as if he had a stomachache.

→ In fact, he _____ a stomachache.

6 He talked as if he could read my mind.

→ In fact, he _____ my mind.

C 괄호 안의 말을 활용하여 문장을 완성하시오.

1 그 소식이 사실이라면 좋을 텐데. (be)

→ I wish the news _____ true.

2 어제 내가 더 열심히 공부했더라면 좋았을 텐데. (study)

→ I wish I _____ harder last night.

3 John은 마치 어른인 것처럼 행동한다. (사실은 그렇지 않음) (be)

→ John acts as if he _____ an adult.

4 Jane은 마치 방금 마라톤을 끝낸 것처럼 피곤함을 느꼈다. (사실은 그렇지 않음) (finish)

→ Jane felt tired as if she _____ just _____ a marathon.

[1~2] 빈칸에 알맞은 것을 고르시오.

01

> What _____ you do if you were invisible?

① would   ② were   ③ will

④ do   ⑤ can

02

> John didn't see the accident himself. But he talks as if he _____ it.

① sees   ② saw

③ has seen   ④ had seen

⑤ would see

[3~4] 주어진 말을 이용하여 우리말과 뜻이 같도록 할 때 빈칸에 알맞은 것을 고르시오.

03

> 내가 어제 그 TV 다큐멘터리를 보았다면 좋았을 텐데.
> I wish I _____ the TV documentary yesterday.

① watch   ② watched

③ has watched   ④ had watched

⑤ would watch

04

> 그는 자신이 마치 모든 것을 아는 것처럼 행동한다.
> He acts as if he _____ everything.

① knows   ② knew

③ has known   ④ had known

⑤ would have known

[5~7] 다음 대화를 읽고 빈칸에 들어갈 알맞은 말을 고르시오.

05

> A: I am sorry that the Lions lost the game.
> B: Yeah. If they _____ the game, they would have played in the championship game.

① wins   ② won   ③ would win

④ have won   ⑤ had won

06

> A: Shall we go out to dinner tonight?
> B: I _____ I could, but I have something important to do today.

① can   ② want

③ wish   ④ will be going to

⑤ had better

07

> A: I wish I had a nice computer that runs very fast. This one is too slow!
> B: I am sorry to hear that.
> A: If I _____ enough money, I will buy a new computer.

① save   ② saved   ③ would save

④ have saved   ⑤ have saved

[8~9] 우리말과 뜻이 같도록 주어진 말을 이용하여 조건에 맞는 문장을 완성하시오. (필요하면 형태를 바꾸시오.)

08 서술형

> 우산이 없었다면, 나는 젖었을 텐데.
> (have, get, 가정법 과거완료)

→ If I _____ an umbrella,

I _____ wet.

09 서술형

내가 키가 조금 더 크다면, 찬장의 과자그릇을 꺼낼 수 있을 텐데. (be, take, 가정법 과거)

→ If I _____ taller, I _____ _____ down the cookie jar from the cupboard.

10 대화의 흐름상 빈칸에 알맞은 말을 고르면?

A: Who is your role model?
B: My role model is Yuna Kim.
_____.

① I wish I could go to Mars.
② I wish I could swim fast.
③ I wish I could run very fast.
④ I wish I could go out to eat.
⑤ I wish I could skate like her.

11 어법상 어색한 것은?

① If she were here, she could help me.
② If I were not busy, I could go with you.
③ He would get angry if he heard the news.
④ I wish I could play soccer like David Beckham.
⑤ She would be disappointed if you don't go to her party.

12 다음 두 문장이 같은 뜻이 되도록 할 때 잘못된 것은?

① He acts as if he were a teacher.
   → In fact, he is not a teacher.
② I wish I could wait for you.
   → I am sorry that I can't wait for you.
③ I wish I had left home earlier.
   → I am sorry that I don't leave home earlier.
④ If we were 19 years old, we could watch the movie.
   → As we are not 19 years old, we can't watch the movie.
⑤ If I were hungry, I would have a meal with you now.
   → As I am not hungry, I will not have a meal with you now.

13 다음 대화 중 자연스럽지 않은 것은?

① A: Your little sister keeps crying.
   B: Yeah. I wish she were quiet.
② A: Are you alright? You look worried.
   B: I got a bad grade in math. I wish I had studied harder.
③ A: Peter is so proud of his winning the contest.
   B: He sure is! He acts as if he were the king of the world.
④ A: Did you know that Jane planned to leave for America?
   B: No, I didn't. If I had known it, I would have told you.
⑤ A: Why don't we go see a movie?
   B: I am too busy right now. If I had not been busy, I would have gone with you.

14 밑줄 친 부분이 어법상 올바른 것은?

① I wish I <u>had been</u> in Paris now.

② She acts as if she <u>had been</u> a famous actor, but she isn't.

③ If you <u>practiced</u> harder, you wouldn't have made such a mistake.

④ If we <u>had had</u> enough time, we could have visited the museum then.

⑤ He talks as if he <u>got</u> the correct answer, but he didn't.

15 주어진 문장을 가정법으로 고친 것 중 틀린 것은?

① He isn't rich, so he can't buy a big house.
  → If he were rich, he can buy a big house.

② He doesn't know the answer, so he can't write it on the board.
  → If he knew the answer, he could write it on the board.

③ I don't have enough money, so I can't buy a pair of nice shoes.
  → If I had enough money, I could buy a pair of nice shoes.

④ As my grandparents don't live near my house, I can't visit them often.
  → If my grandparents lived near my house, I could visit them often.

⑤ He has to finish his group work by this weekend, so he is busy.
  → If he didn't have to finish his group work this weekend, he wouldn't be busy.

[16~18] 다음 문장을 가정법을 사용하여 다시 쓰시오.

16 서술형

Yumi is sick, so she can't come to school.

→ If Yumi _____,
  she _____ to school.

17 서술형

My father had to work last weekend, so he was not happy.

→ If he _____ last weekend,
  he _____ happy.

18 서술형

I am sorry that my mom is so strict.

→ I wish that my mom _____
  _____ so strict.

19 다음 중 어법상 옳은 문장으로 짝지어진 것은?

ⓐ He acts as if he were a superman.

ⓑ If she were old enough, she could go to school.

ⓒ If it had rained, the flower could have got enough water.

ⓓ She talks as if she has traveled to Italy last year, but she has never traveled there.

ⓔ I wish I had been in New York now to see the Statue of Liberty.

① ⓐ, ⓑ, ⓒ   ② ⓐ, ⓒ, ⓓ   ③ ⓐ, ⓒ, ⓔ
④ ⓑ, ⓒ, ⓓ   ⑤ ⓒ, ⓓ, ⓔ

20 다음 중 어법상 잘못된 ⓐ~ⓔ문장을 바르게 고친 학생 두 명을 고르면?

> ⓐ I wish I live near my school now.
> ⓑ If he doesn't know where I am, he couldn't find me.
> ⓒ If she had a cell phone, I can call her.
> ⓓ He acts as if he was the captain of our school basketball team.
> ⓔ He would have been caught in rain if he have stayed longer.

① Linda : ⓐ에서 'live'를 'will live'로 고쳐야 해.
② Mike : ⓑ에서 'doesn't'를 'didn't'로 고쳐야 해.
③ John : ⓒ에서 'call'을 'called'로 고쳐야 해.
④ Jane : ⓓ에서 'was'를 'were'로 고쳐야 해.
⑤ Hanna : ⓔ에서 'have stayed'를 'has stayed' 로 고쳐야 해.

21 ⓐ~ⓒ에 들어갈 알맞은 말이 순서대로 바르게 짝지어진 것은?

> A: Have you met John, who came to our school as an exchange student?
> B: No, I haven't had a chance to yet.
> A: He speaks Korean as if he ⓐ _____ a Korean!
> B: Really? I wish I ⓑ _____ a chance to meet him.
> A: If you heard him speak Korean, you ⓒ _____ your ears.

① is, have, would believe
② was, had, wouldn't have believed
③ were, had had, wouldn't believe
④ was, had had, would have believed
⑤ were, had, will not believe

[22~23] 밑줄 친 부분에서 어법상 틀린 곳을 찾아 바르게 고쳐 쓰시오.

22 서술형

> If we lived in space, <u>we would have become taller.</u>

틀린 곳: _____ → _____

23 서술형

> If she had learned Spanish, <u>she could understand what they told her yesterday.</u>

틀린 곳: _____ → _____

24 다음 밑줄 친 ⓐ~ⓔ중 어법상 틀린 것은?

> It was getting dark and raining cats and dogs. A traveler was walking in a field and looking for shelter from the rain without success. He thought, "I wish I ⓐ <u>were</u> at home." He felt sorry that he had promised to visit his friend that day. If he ⓑ <u>hadn't promised</u>, he ⓒ <u>wouldn't have left</u> his home. He thought, "If I don't visit him today, he ⓓ <u>will</u> be very disappointed." Then, he saw a light from a house at the end of the road. He was delighted as if he ⓔ <u>had seen</u> his friend's house.

① ⓐ   ② ⓑ   ③ ⓒ   ④ ⓓ   ⑤ ⓔ

25 서술형 심화

Fill in the blanks using the given words.

A: Are you all right? What's wrong?
B: I missed the train for London. I have
   to get there by 4 o'clock.
A: Hmmm. If you (1) ＿＿＿＿＿＿
   (come) five minutes earlier, you
   (2) ＿＿＿＿＿＿ (miss) it.
B: I know. I wish I (3) ＿＿＿＿＿＿
   (leave) home earlier.
A: If you (4) ＿＿＿＿＿＿ (come) back
   in an hour, you can catch the next
   train to London.
B: I see. Thanks.

(1) → ＿＿＿＿＿＿＿＿＿＿

(2) → ＿＿＿＿＿＿＿＿＿＿

(3) → ＿＿＿＿＿＿＿＿＿＿

(4) → ＿＿＿＿＿＿＿＿＿＿

부 록

A. 불규칙동사 변화표

B. 형용사/부사의 형태 변화

C. by 이외의 전치사를 사용하는 수동태 표현

A. 불규칙동사 변화표

원형	과거형	과거분사형	뜻
arise	arose	arisen	생겨나다
awake	awoke	awoken	깨어나다
bear	bore	born	참다, 낳다
become	became	become	~가 되다
begin	began	begun	시작하다
behold	beheld	beheld	주시하다
bend	bent	bent	구부리다
bite	bit	bitten	물다
blow	blew	blown	폭파하다
break	broke	broken	깨다
bring	brought	brought	가져오다
build	built	built	짓다
burn	burnt	burnt	태우다
buy	bought	bought	사다
catch	caught	caught	잡다
choose	chose	chosen	고르다
cost	cost	cost	(값이) ~들다
cut	cut	cut	자르다
deal	dealt	dealt	다루다
dig	dug	dug	파다
draw	drew	drawn	그리다, 당기다
drink	drank	drunk	마시다
drive	drove	driven	운전하다
fall	fell	fallen	떨어지다
feed	fed	fed	먹이다

원형	과거형	과거분사형	뜻
feel	felt	felt	느끼다
fight	fought	fought	싸우다
find	found	found	발견하다
flee	fled	fled	도망치다
fly	flew	flown	날다
forbid	forbade	forbidden	금지하다
forget	forgot	forgotten	잊다
forgive	forgave	forgiven	용서하다
found	founded	founded	설립하다
freeze	froze	frozen	얼리다
get	got	gotten/got	얻다
give	gave	given	주다
grow	grew	grown	자라다
hang	hung	hung	매달다
have	had	had	가지다, 먹다
hear	heard	heard	듣다
hide	hid	hidden	숨기다
hit	hit	hit	치다
hold	held	held	잡다, 개최하다
hurt	hurt	hurt	부상 입히다
keep	kept	kept	유지하다
know	knew	known	알다
lay	laid	laid	놓다
lead	led	led	이끌다
lean	leaned/leant	leaned/leant	기울다

원형	과거형	과거분사형	뜻
leave	left	left	떠나다
lend	lent	lent	빌려주다
let	let	let	놓다
lie	lied	lied	거짓말하다
lie	lay	lain	눕다
light	lit	lit	밝히다
lose	lost	lost	잃다
make	made	made	만들다
mean	meant	meant	의미하다
meet	met	met	만나다
mistake	mistook	mistaken	실수하다
outrun	outran	outrun	앞지르다
overcome	overcame	overcome	극복하다
pay	paid	paid	지불하다
prove	proved	proved/proven	증명하다
put	put	put	놓다
raise	raised	raised	~를 올리다
read	read	read	읽다
ride	rode	ridden	타다
ring	rang	rung	종을 울리다
rise	rose	risen	오르다
run	ran	run	뛰다
say	said	said	말하다
see	saw	seen	보다
sell	sold	sold	팔다

원형	과거형	과거분사형	뜻
send	sent	sent	보내다
set	set	set	정하다
shake	shook	shaken	흔들다
shut	shut	shut	닫다
sing	sang	sung	노래하다
sit	sat	sat	앉다
sleep	slept	slept	자다
slide	slid	slid	미끄러지다
spend	spent	spent	소비하다
spill	spilt	spilt	엎지르다
split	split	split	쪼개다
spoil	spoiled /spoilt	spoiled /spoilt	망치다
spread	spread	spread	퍼지다
stand	stood	stood	서다
steal	stole	stolen	훔치다
swear	swore	sworn	맹세하다
sweep	swept	swept	싹 쓸다
take	took	taken	가지고 가다
teach	taught	taught	가르치다
tear	tore	torn	찢다
tell	told	told	말하다
think	thought	thought	생각하다
wake	woke	woken	깨우다
wear	wore	worn	입다
write	wrote	written	쓰다

B. 형용사/부사의 형태 변화

1. 규칙 변화

	비교급	최상급	원급 – 비교급 – 최상급
대부분의 경우	-er (-e로 끝나는 단어는 -r)	-est (-e로 끝나는 단어는 -st)	tall – taller – tallest large – larger – largest
〈단모음 + 자음〉로 끝나는 단어	자음 한 번 더 쓰고 -er	자음 한 번 더 쓰고 -est	big – bigger – biggest
〈자음 + y〉로 끝나는 단어	-y를 -ier로	-y를 -iest로	pretty – prettier – prettiest
2음절 이상 혹은 -ful, -ous, -ing 등으로 끝나는 단어	앞에 more를 붙인다	앞에 most를 붙인다	beautiful – more beautiful – most beautiful

2. 불규칙 변화

원급	비교급	최상급	뜻
good	better	best	좋은
well			(형) 건강한 / (부) 잘
bad	worse	worst	나쁜
ill			병든, 나쁜
many/much	more	most	(수) 많은 / (양) 많은
little	less	least	(양) 적은
old	older	oldest	나이 든, 오래 된
	elder	eldest	연상의
late	later	latest	늦은
	latter	last	나중의
far	farther	farthest	(거리) 먼
	further	furthest	(정도) 더욱

C. by 이외의 전치사를 사용하는 수동태 표현

be surprised at	~에 놀라다	be pleased with	~에 기뻐하다
be known to	~에게 알려져 있다	be bored with	~에 싫증나다
be known as	~로서 알려져 있다 (자격)	be tired of	~에 싫증나다
be known for	~때문에 알려져 있다 (이유)	be scared of	~을 두려워하다
be made of/from	~으로 만들어지다	be prepared for	~에 대해 준비되다
be interested in	~에 관심 있다	be filled with	~으로 가득 차다
be satisfied with	~에 만족하다	be dressed in	~으로 차려 입다

비법 담은 중학 영문법

Answer Key

영문법

특강편

2

비법 담은 중학 영문법

법 은 학

영문법

Answer Key

특강편 2

Chapter 01 문장의 형식

핵심만 콕! 문법 Check

Point 1-4

A
1. looked
2. a ghost
3. terrible
4. smell
5. sounds
6. good
7. soft
8. tastes

B
1. nervous
2. strange
3. good
4. great

C
1. He gave his email address to me.
2. Julie made some chocolate for me.
3. Penny asked a favor of me.

D
1. My younger sister cooks delicious food for me.
2. I will buy her some flowers.

Point 5-8

A
1. hold
2. go
3. to clean
4. touch
5. break
6. to take

B
1. to help
2. to come
3. to use
4. to give

C
1. She will order them to send the packages.
2. Mary asked Tom to be quiet in the library.
3. I had them apologize to each other.

D
1. do the laundry
2. me to start the job again
3. He heard me call his name.

내신 만점! 실전 기출

01. ⑤　　02. ③　　03. for　　04. of
05. ③　　06. ③, ④　07. ④　　08. ①
09. play, to play　　10. ④　　11. ②
12. He made me fix his computer.
13. never to be late
14. ③　　15. ③　　16. ⑤　　17. ④
18. We helped the children to cook.
19. I saw Matt talking on the phone an hour ago.

20. ③　　　21. makes me happy
22. You look very happy, bought me a new cellphone
23. told Jinsu not to bring food
24. told him not to keep the window open
25. (1) ⓒ feeling → feel
　　(2) ⓔ to you a letter
　　　→ you a letter 또는 a letter to you

Chapter 02 to부정사

핵심만 콕! 문법 Check

Point 1-3

A
1. To talk
2. to be
3. to see
4. not to send the letter

B
1. to study
2. to pass
3. to ask

C
1. It is fun to hang out with friends.
2. It is not easy to be a famous singer.
3. when I should leave
4. how she should fly

D
1. wants to be
2. what to do
3. where to go
4. decided not to go

Point 4-7

A
1. to go
2. nothing to show
3. to write on
4. to live in

B
1. 결과　　2. 감정의 원인　　3. 판단의 근거

C
1. as to catch
2. order to win
3. order not to fail

D
1. lived to be 120
2. something to drink
3. to play with
4. came to school to meet

A 1. of   2. for   3. for   4. of

B 1. so weak that he can't carry

     2. so short that she couldn't reach

C 1. so strong that I can lift

     2. so rich that he could buy

D 1. so big(large) that I can't wear

     2. for her to answer

     3. too hot to eat

     4. fast enough to

내신 만점! 실전 기출

01. ②   **02.** ②   **03.** with   **04.** ④

05. too suprised to move   **06.** ②

07. (1) so, that, she, can't

     (2) so, that, he, can

08. ③   **09.** ②   **10.** ③   **11.** ②

12. how to save money wisely   **13.** ①

14. to buy some bananas

15. ③   **16.** ④, ⑤

17. (1) something warm to wear

     (2) a pen, write with

18. It is rude to talk on the phone loudly

19. ①, ⑤   **20.** ⑤

21. Daniel went to the hospital to see a doctor.

22. (1) studies hard so as to pass the exam

     (2) exercises every day in order to stay fit

23. ④   **24.** ②

25. was too weak to lift the chair,

     is strong enough to lift it

Chapter 03 동명사

핵심만 콕! 문법 Check

Point 1-3

A 1. becoming   2. Making, To make

     3. helping, to help   4. my, me

B 1. going   2. painting

     3. running   4. playing

C 1. My goal is waking up early

     2. Playing badminton is

     3. Riding a bike with friends is

     4. is winning the school speech contest

D 1. not being

     2. mind my(me) sitting

     3. interested in making

     4. wish to have

Point 4-6

A 1. camping   2. fixing   3. getting up

     4. to live   5. visiting   6. buying

     7. going

B 1. to win   2. writing   3. to visit

     4. singing   5. to travel   6. closing

     7. to buy

C 1. stop wasting   2. gave up catching

     3. decided to exercise   4. avoided meeting

     5. stopped to pick   6. forgot giving

     7. waste, watching

내신 만점! 실전 기출

01. ③   **02.** ①   **03.** ②

04. to go, going

05. ⑤   **06.** ④   **07.** ③

08. to hang   **09** staying up

10. ②   **11.** ③

12. What about watching a movie

13. ⑤   **14.** ②   **15.** ⑤

16. (1) remembers buying (2) forgot to water
17. ②　　　　**18.** ③　　　**19.** ③　　　**20.** ①
21. ③　　　　　**22.** getting up regularly is important
23. Thank you for hepling me find my lost puppy.
24. to ride a bike without falling
25. (1) am good at doing voices
　　　 (2) I look forward to hearing from you

Chapter 04 분사

핵심만 콕! 문법 Check

Point 1-3

A	1. singing	2. sitting	3. built
B	1. painted	2. broken	3. cooked
	4. called		
C	1. barking	2. amazing	3. used
D	1. satisfying, satisfied		
	2. shocking, shocked		

Point 4-6

A	1. 현재분사　　2. 동명사　　3. 동명사
B	1. Finishing her work
	2. Studying hard
	3. Cleaning the room
C	1. When he saw us
	2. Because he was late
	3. If he leaves right now
D	1. Waiting for our turn
	2. Feeling sleepy

내신 만점! 실전 기출

01. ③　　　　　**02.** ③
03. The woman standing at the door
04. ②　　　　**05.** ②　　　**06.** ④
07. flying a kite
08. ②　　　　**09.** ②　　　**10.** ③

11. ⑤　　　**12.** ③　　　**13.** ①　　　**14.** ④
15. Being　　**16.** After it was fixed
17. ④　　　**18.** ①　　　**19.** ④　　　**20.** ③, ⑤
21. ③　　　**22.** ⑤
23. Used properly, the machine will help you a lot.
24. ②
25. (1) Reading English books an hour a day
　　　 (2) Promising to go home together
　　　 (3) Cooking well

Chapter 05 시제

핵심만 콕! 문법 Check

Point 1, 2

A	1. heard	2. rises	3. won
	4. rides	5. have	
B	1. runs	2. freezes	3. are
	4. lost	5. told	
	6. am going to finish		
C	1. look → looking	2. meant → means	
	3. is thinking → thinks	4. comes → coming	
	5. thinks → is thinking		
D	1. Have you seen	2. Are you having	
	3. do you think		

Point 3-6

A	1. have been	2. hasn't finished
	3. has been	4. has been
B	1. has gone to	2. has learned, for
	3. has been to	4. has just finished
C	1. have lived	2. ate
	3. went	4. were you
	5. has never caught	6. O
D	1. Have you made	
	2. Has Jane lived in Japan	
	3. has never been to Namdaemun Market before	
	4. What have you done since this morning	
	5. has not finished his homework yet	

01. will not use 02. ③   03. ④   04. ②
05. ②   06. ④   07. has lived, for
08. has just finished cleaning his room
09. ①, ④   10. ①   11. ④   12. ④
13. ①   14. ⑤   15. ①
16. They have not arrived in Seoul yet.
17. ⑤   18. ③   19. ②   20. ①, ⑤
21. ②   22. ④   23. ②
24. has cleaned the living room, hasn't bought any
     snacks
25. (1) has gained
     (2) is going to walk / will walk

Chapter 06 관계사

핵심만 콕! 문법 Check

A   1. who   2. whose
    3. which   4. that
B   1. who   2. whose
    3. which   4. that
C   1. X   2. X   3. O   4. X
    5. X   6. X   7. O
D   1. that glitters
    2. that can teach Korean
    3. whose(of which) cover is black

A   1. which   2. whose
    3. who(m)   4. whose
    5. which   6. who
    7. who(m)
B   1. what   2. what   3. what you want
C   1. I gave to him   2. John really likes
    3. written in English   4. I talked to
    5. what he said   6. the things that are

A   1. at which, where   2. at which, when
    3. why   4. how, the way
B   1. O   2. which/that
    3. how 삭제   4. which
    5. which   6. there 삭제
C   1. when I do
    2. where he jogs
    3. the reason for which he was late for school
    4. how I could make a copy
    5. when she was

01. ①   02. which   03. ③   04. ②
05. ①   06. which(that) we don't finish
07. The movie that(which) I watched yesterday
     was interesting.
08. ④   09. ④   10. ④
11. (1) which(that) is, (2) who(that) are
12. ③   13. ③   14. What he wanted
15. ②, ④   16. ③   17. ④
18. where my father works
19. That is how she makes carrot cake
20. ③   21. ②   22. ②   23. ①, ⑤
24. Tell me the time when we can go there.
25. (1) an animal which(that) has lived with people
         for a long time
     (2) a language which(that) people in France
         speak
     (3) a house which(that) we can see in Alaska

Chapter 07 수동태

Point 1-3

A 1. be done   2. is fed   3. is loved
    4. fixed   5. was written   6. ordered

B 1. was washed   2. were destroyed
    3. will be made

C 1. is spoken   2. was invented
    3. was sung

D 1. These products were not made in Korea.
    2. Was this computer fixed by him?
    3. Are these rooms cleaned every day?

Point 4-9

A 1. Some chocolate were made for me by Yuna.
    2. A love letter was sent to her by someone.
    3. He was elected president by them.

B 1. was given some allowance by his mom
    2. were given to Peter by his mom
    3. was told to him by us

C 1. The puppy was looked after by mom.
    2. He should not be looked down on by them.
    3. Her grandmother was taken care of by Jenny.

D 1. in   2. at   3. with
    4. of   5. to

내신 만점! 실전 기출

01. ④   **02.** are enjoyed   **03.** ③
04. ③   **05.** ④
06. The homework must be completed by this Friday.
07. ④   **08.** ③
09. were brought up by   **10.** ③   **11.** ⑤
12. ④   **13.** ④   **14.** ④   **15.** ②
16. Eating food should not be allowed
17. ①   **18.** ⑤   **19.** ⑤   **20.** ③
21. The bread was baked by me.   **22.** ④
23. ⓐ A new 007 movie will be released soon.
    ⓑ I was deeply impressed.
24. ⓐ is located   ⓑ is known to   ⓒ is held
25. (1) was filled with
     (2) were covered with

Chapter 08 가정법

Point 1, 2

A 1. were   2. is
    3. had   4. had had
    5. have practiced   6. had known
    7. have known   8. have finished

B 1. am not, can't
    2. doesn't like, doesn't ask
    3. weren't, couldn't join
    4. rained, wasn't held
    5. watered, didn't die

C 1. is
    2. couldn't have finished
    3. had had
    4. could do
    5. would have stayed
    6. hadn't cleaned

Point 3, 4

A 1. had done   2. were
    3. had been   4. hadn't fought

B 1. I were not   2. I knew
    3. I didn't join   4. melted
    5. doesn't have   6. couldn't read

C 1. were   2. had studied
    3. were   4. had, finished

내신 만점! 실전 기출

01. ①   **02.** ④   **03.** ④   **04.** ②
05. ⑤   **06.** ③   **07.** ①
08. hadn't had, would have got
09. were, could take
10. ⑤   **11.** ⑤   **12.** ③   **13.** ⑤
14. ④   **15.** ①
16. were not sick, could come
17. hadn't had to work, would have been
18. were not

19. ①   **20.** ②, ④   **21.** ③

22. have become → become

23. understand → have understood

24. ⑤

25. (1) had come

(2) wouldn't have missed

(3) had left

(4) come

MEMO

단기간에 마무리하는 8가지 핵심 비법 **특강편**